HIGHER *life* DESIGN

D1052424

Praise for *Higher Life Design*

"Jefferson has raised the flag for a new generation of entrepreneurs, empowered to amplify their interests and passions with businesses that support amazing lifestyles. In addition to realizing this dream himself, Jefferson has succeeded in training hundreds of thousands of others to do the same. Let him be your guide on this amazing journey!"

—Jesse Krieger, best selling author of
Lifestyle Entrepreneur

"Jefferson is a doer and a go-getter! He doesn't just think about what he wants. He sets his sites on it and hits it every time. You hold the perfect guidebook to get to places you've never been. Follow Jefferson's story and then follow the steps he lays out for you. You've waited long enough."

—Dr. Wayne D Pernell, PhD, High Performance Leadership Coach and author of *Choosing Your Power*

"Jefferson's passion comes pouring through these pages. He equips and inspires you to achieve greater health, wealth, and happiness by helping you design a Higher Life."

—Marcia Wieder, CEO/Founder, Dream University

"For the vast majority of us that seek rapid success in all areas of our lives, based on timeless principles, *Higher Life Design* offers a uniquely holistic approach that is refreshingly easy to read, and more importantly, easy to recall. I will enthusiastically share this book, and use the framework presented by Jefferson, to build teams of powerful individuals seeking to get off the ground and soar at the highest levels of success...quickly!"

—Wayne Nugent CVO & Founder of WorldVentures

HIGHER
life
DESIGN

ARRIVING AT YOUR INTENDED DESTINATION
HEALTHY, WEALTHY, AND HAPPY

JEFFERSON SANTOS

NEW YORK

HIGHER *life* DESIGN
Arriving at Your Intended Destination Healthy, Wealthy, and Happy

Published in New York, New York, by Morgan James Publishing. Morgan James and The Entrepreneurial Publisher are trademarks of Morgan James, LLC.
www.MorganJamesPublishing.com

The Morgan James Speakers Group can bring authors to your live event. For more information or to book an event visit The Morgan James Speakers Group at www.TheMorganJamesSpeakersGroup.com.

To protect the privacy of those who have shared their stories with the author, some details and names have been changed.

The Internet addresses, email addresses, and phone numbers in this book are accurate at the time of publication. They are provided as a resource. Morgan James does not endorse them or vouch for their content or permanence.

Published in association with Kary Oberbrunner—Redeem the Day, P.O. Box 43 Powell, OH, 4065, www.karyoberbrunner.com

Higher Life Design, Higher Life Design Travelers, The Attitude Equation, The Integration Effect, The Hunger Triad, The Four Fuel Groups, The Act Up System, The First Class Five, The First Class Formula, and The Higher Life Design Manifesto are trademarks of Jefferson Santos.

A FREE eBook edition is available with the purchase of this print book

CLEARLY PRINT YOUR NAME IN THE BOX ABOVE

Instructions to claim your free eBook edition:
1. Download the BitLit app for Android or iOS
2. Write your name in UPPER CASE in the box
3. Use the BitLit app to submit a photo
4. Download your eBook to any device

ISBN 978-1-63047-133-0 paperback
ISBN 978-1-63047-134-7 eBook
ISBN 978-1-63047-135-4 audio
ISBN 978-1-63047-136-1 hardcover
Library of Congress Control Number:
2014933861

Cover Design by:
Kristian Bottini

Interior Design by:
Bonnie Bushman
bonnie@caboodlegraphics.com

Get involved today, visit
www.MorganJamesBuilds.com.

Habitat for Humanity®
Peninsula and
Greater Williamsburg
Building Partner

For Megan, Harrison, and Livingston
You've made my life unimaginably
better than even my wildest dreams.

CONTENTS

"A master in the art of living draws no sharp distinction between his work and his play; his labor and his leisure; his mind and his body; his education and his recreation. He hardly knows which is which. He simply pursues his vision of excellence through whatever he is doing, and leaves others to determine whether he is working or playing. To himself, he always appears to be doing both."

— **L. P. Jacks**[1]

Introduction:
My Assassin, the Mailbox

We don't get what we want;
we get who we are

I have always had a grand vision of what I wanted my life to look like. When I met Jefferson, I knew God had blessed me with a mentor and friend who could give my vision color and provide guidance on making that vision a reality.

Very rarely in life do we have the opportunity to meet genuine people who inspire others; who give without expecting anything in return. Jefferson is that person.

— **Clement Boyd**

I walked down the sidewalk on that Dallas afternoon filled with fear. Mustering every ounce of courage, I prepared for the worst. This was the part of my day I hated most.

Some people might see my destination as a place of possibilities. I saw it as a place of pain. Trust me, this wasn't my favorite place to frequent. I'd rather be found in a gym doing 60 minutes of CrossFit strength and endurance training than at the apartment mailbox for even 60 seconds.

Rather than a friend, the mailbox felt like a deadly assassin. Its favorite targets?

My pride.

My future.

And most devastating—my credit score.

I wasn't financially *irresponsible*, but Dave Ramsey wasn't sitting at my feet to learn any tips about money management either.

The truth is, I was broke. Worse than that, I was broke *and* in the hole. My bank account was in the red: -$1,100. My debt load told a similar story: $70,000. Despite a large amount of entrepreneurial ambition for my new start-up business, life had me in a choke hold. Yep. I was 23 years old, more than $70K in debt, and living with my mom in her apartment. I was the essence of a self-made man. Except, I hadn't *made* anything yet and I definitely didn't feel like a man at the moment.

A boy?

Perhaps—but a boy with a big dream nonetheless.

My debt wasn't from impulsive spending. It was forged with endless energy and attempted strategy. I had jumped into several businesses with an uncommon amount of zeal. Never wanting to do anything halfway, I made these businesses my lifestyle. I blended work and play into one big goal, except that this particular goal found pleasure in eluding my best attempts.

My Impending Storm on the Horizon

With an overcast Texas sky heavy with humidity, two inevitable realities loomed on the horizon—rain and ruin. Undoubtedly, two storms were brewing—one involving the weather and the other involving my future.

As my thoughts raced about my impending financial failure, I pushed the door open to the corridor with the mailboxes. My eyes scanned the top row for my box…or more accurately put, my *mom's* box. I prayed for junk mail—at least that type didn't have an invoice or a bill attached to it.

The entire hallway felt hellish. Used gum on the floor mimicked a type of minefield. One wrong step and I'd be cleaning off unwanted debris from my worn out pair of Asics. Nike shoes might have ruled the day, but certainly not my budget. I wanted to make it to the age of 25 without a debtor's prison sentence.

Dodging landmines pretty much encapsulated my feeling at that moment. I constantly felt stalked by bill collectors. Wasn't this supposed to be the land of the free and the home of the brave?

That wasn't the home I knew.

And I didn't feel brave *or* free for that matter.

I lived in a different reality. Rather than the land of fulfillment, I found myself taking up residence in a land called frustration. And more than just a citizen, I felt like the mayor of this unlucky land.

Still, I never considered quitting. Though I was down at the moment, I wasn't about to accept defeat. The last few months, I even got a little creative in my attempt to score a payoff. Although I won a few "best chest" contests at the local night clubs, the $200 first prize didn't come close to closing my financial gap.

Until this point in my life, I had focused on trying to change the wrong thing. Unaware of my faulty strategy, I spent my energy on reversing my results. Little did I know the flaw in that thinking.

At that time, I thought *we got what we wanted*. But since then, I've realized *we get who we are*. Trying to change our results without first trying to change ourselves is like trying to drive a car without any gas. It gets us nowhere fast. I didn't need anyone to convince me my life was headed nowhere.

Thankfully, this book isn't about nowhere. Rather, it's about somewhere. It's about arriving at your intended destination healthy, wealthy, and happy.

Today, my mailbox is once again a place of potential rather than a place of pain. Instead of bills, I regularly find stacks of checks. I don't live with my mom anymore or in an apartment for that matter. Quite the opposite, I've designed a completely different life—the Higher Life Design to be exact.

Meet My Difference Maker

Friends who knew me back in my apartment days often ask how I made the transition. They wonder if luck or chance had something to do with it.

To their surprise, luck and chance didn't have *anything* to do with it.

The truth is that I discovered a process I call the Higher Life Design. These seven steps enabled me to increase my health, wealth, and happiness. I changed my results by first changing my design.

This process helped me earn several million dollars and build a team of well over 100,000 leaders in more than 30 countries. I've since travelled the world and taken 107 vacations in 84 months. I've trained teams from New York to Singapore; Amsterdam to Zimbabwe and everywhere else in between. I've been blessed to share the stage with some of the biggest names in my industry—Dani Johnson, Brendon Burchard, Marcia Wieder, Cynthia Kersey, Loral Langemeier, Les Brown and Peter Diamandis.

More importantly, I've been able to build schools in Guatemala and other regions in desperate need of resources. Through "VolunTourism" I've been able to give my time, talent, and treasures to people who need a hand up, not a hand out.

If you would have told me this back at my mom's mailbox on that overcast Dallas day I wouldn't have believed you.

The rest of this book is that reality—the Higher Life Design revealed. I'll be your guide. Together, we'll take a transformational trip and explore the attitudes, skills, and practices that make up Higher Life Design Travelers.

Along the way you'll experience new results, new life, and maybe even a new destination.

Here's what I mean:

- **New Results:** It's about taking your results—no matter how good or bad—and transforming them into more than you can even imagine.
- **New Life:** It's about significantly increasing your health, wealth, and happiness through 7 proven steps.
- **New Destination:** It's about arriving at your newly designed destination.

Be prepared though. The trip we're about to take is only for people who are hungry for more.

Call it a hunch, but because you're reading this book, I have a strong inkling you're one of those people.

PART I

TAKEOFF—*EXPECTATION*

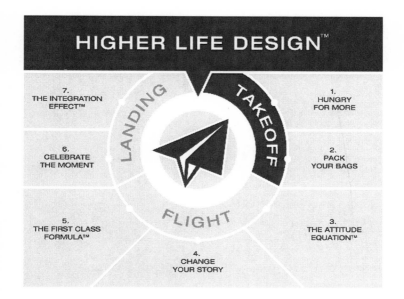

Step One:
Hungry for More

Your influence increases in direct proportion to your appetite

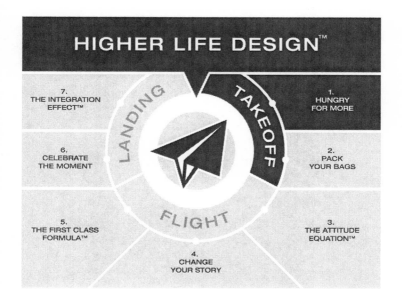

I worked hard becoming a top realtor who earns lots of money. However, life is more than just earning money. It's about designing and creating a happy and fulfilling life. Jefferson has truly increased my life through his friendship and mentorship. He's dramatically increased my appetite to become a better father, husband, son, friend, and servant leader through his 'lead by example' approach.

— **Joe T.**

From the time I met Jefferson more than three years ago, I've been incredibly impressed with how he carries himself. Jefferson not only Designed a Higher Life for himself, but he's also helped others create the same success in their own lives.

Although I was already successful within my industry, I wanted to step up my game in other areas. Jefferson helped me overcome my own ignorance and see the power of personal development. I know a Higher Life is now possible.

Jefferson is an authentic student who pours his knowledge into others—like me. For that, I'm forever grateful.

— **Toby L.**

"I get that car," I told my fellow compadre.

My friend and I loved hopping in exquisite and expensive vehicles at a high-end restaurant near our house. Our hobby was completely legal; that summer we worked as valets—not carjackers.

Back then, parking these cars seemed to be as close as I'd ever come to a little piece of automotive paradise. I particularly enjoyed the Mercedes S Class and BMW 7 series.

"Fine, but I get the next good one," my friend shot back.

Following his reply, *my* car—or at least the one I got dibs on—rolled right up to me in front of the restaurant. It wore a fresh coat of wax and sported shiny rims. No one could convince me otherwise—this car had my name on it.

This car's owner didn't need any instructions. He let me open the door for his passenger first, himself second. Then he handed me a tip. We call this type of driver an "insider"—one who understands valet etiquette.

Today, we have websites like *The Art of Manliness* that help alleviate any ignorance. I found the post, "How to Use Valet Parking (Without Looking Like an Idiot)" educationally entertaining. Judging by the number of "Likes" on Facebook, others found it beneficial, too.[2]

Many people view the valet profession with a deep sort of mystique. Think about it. You pull up to a complete stranger and then walk away from your car with the keys in the ignition and the engine still running. Typically, cars are your second most valuable physical possession. Yet, in this situation you simply abandon it. Crazier yet, you *actually pay* the valet to take your car away!

Strange, I know. But once I slid into the driver's seat, there was nothing strange about it. I felt perfectly at home.

Sitting behind the wheel, all five of my senses immediately ignited.

I *felt* the power of the engine when I touched the gas pedal.

I *heard* the adrenalized music pumping through the state-of-the-art sound system.

I *smelled* the brand new leather spread throughout the rich interior.

I *tasted* a life much different than my own.

I *saw* myself for my potential contribution rather than my present circumstances.

Something in me changed that summer. My awareness increased and I began to ask bigger questions.

Why couldn't I keep up with the clientele at this high-end restaurant?

Why couldn't I go where they went?

Why couldn't I drive what they drove?

Was I simply destined to park their prizes in the parking lot of life or was I meant for more?

I already knew the answers, but at that point in my life it just hadn't manifested yet.

The car alone didn't snap me out of my S-T-U-C-K position. Rather, it's what the car represented.

Financial freedom.

Emotional freedom.

Personal freedom.

For the first time in my life, I saw a fork in the road.

Standing in front of the restaurant, I found myself crouching under the weight of the bills that crushed my creativity. But sitting behind the wheel of that luxury car, I found myself bumping up against the first step in the Higher Life Design.

I found myself hungry for more.

Are you hungry?

Hunger is a word derived from Old English with Germanic roots. It means a "strong desire" and relates to life, not death.[3]

Make no mistake—dead people aren't hungry. In fact, they aren't anything. And because they feel nothing, they *desire* nothing. After all, they're dead!

Living people are different. We *feel* hunger and therefore we *feel* the need to feed our desire. Our appetite pushes us onward.

Notice what we say when we're really hungry. We say we have hunger *pains*. These pains aren't meant to hurt us; they're meant to help us. Hunger pains push us toward action—namely satisfying our stomachs.

The animal kingdom teaches us a powerful lesson about hunger. I remember watching an incredibly breathtaking clip on a nature show.[4] The cameras captured a pack of wolves attacking a herd of buffalo. These beasts clearly outweighed the wolves—2,000 pounds compared to 175 pounds or less. As long as they maintained their ground, the buffalo always maintained the upper hand.

The narrator on this particular show explained that a stand down between these two species can for last days. However, most wolves don't simply *sit* with their hunger. They *act*. Their hunger motivates them toward achieving their goal—namely, their dinner.

Here's the interesting phenomenon.

Wolves only win the battle when they attack from behind. Buffalo flaunt a powerful set of horns proudly attached to their massive heads, yet these horns do nothing if the buffalo aren't facing the wolves. Plenty of wolves have died going head-to-head with buffalo. (Two-foot long horns tend to have that effect.)

Because wolves know this, they work together to scare the buffalo. If they persuade them to run, their chances of eating dramatically improve. In this television program, the buffalo eventually lost their nerve and fled from their adversaries, even though they weighed 10 times more.

In an effort to escape, the buffalo "broke trail." They attempted to sprint through the ungracious snow drifts. By heading through the brush, the buffalo utilized a brilliant strategy and forced the wolves to split up.

The lead wolf's commitment continued, though—his hunger pushing him on. As his pursuit strengthened, so did his odds of a successful hunt. He locked on to his prey and singlehandedly slowed down the mighty beast. After a few minutes, his "hunger for more" paid off with big dividends—measured in buffalo meat.

Feed Your Appetite Using The Hunger Triad

Although you're not a wolf chasing a buffalo, you can still draw several parallels. I refer to these steps as The Hunger Triad. They are: Know Your Hunger, Grow Your Hunger, and Show Your Hunger. Let's unpack them one at a time.

Step One: Know Your Hunger

The wolf knows his hunger. His internal drive energizes and empowers him. He knows resources aren't lying unguarded in the open. Instead, he must locate and appropriate them if he wants to satisfy his hunger.

Similarly, you must feel your own hunger. Apathy isn't an option and plateauing isn't acceptable. Your hunger prepares and propels you to take responsibility for your life. You must locate and utilize resources to satisfy your hunger. Knowing this hunger drives you to action.

Step Two: Grow Your Hunger

The wolf grows his hunger. He doesn't simply attack. He develops a strategy first. By circling his target, he sizes up his competition and adjusts accordingly. As he invests time, the wolf's appetite grows slowly and steadily edging him on and bolstering his bravery.

Similarly, you must grow your hunger. By investing the proper time and energy into exploring the marketplace, your appetite begins to grow. Witnessing best practices and effective methods, your strategy and bravery increase in connection to each other.

Step Three: Show Your Hunger

The wolf shows his hunger. He doesn't simply sit with his plan. Instead, he seizes the moment. He remains focused, then takes advantage of the opportunity at hand. When an angle appears, he exploits it. An industrious student, he waits patiently, and then explodes into action at the right time.

Similarly, you must show your hunger. You can't sit on the sideline and speculate. You must also take action. By maintaining your focus, you can make the most of the moment by pursuing your goal. Embody patience until your opportunity presents itself, then act, knowing that because you've prepared for the moment, your moment is prepared for you.

Higher Life Design Travelers are Made for More

All Higher Life Design Travelers know their hunger is much more than a physical impulse. Their appetites surpass their stomachs and their cravings outpace their palates.

You were made for more:

To be more.

To do more.

To have more.

To give more.

This isn't because you're selfish, but rather because you're human. You were created for a fuller expression and a fuller expansion of your current awareness. Everybody knows this.

Runners want faster times.

Businesses want bigger profits.

Charities want greater impact.

Nobody wants poorer health, smaller wealth, or less happiness. Your desire to increase reminds you that you're created in God's image. This hunger propels you toward action—namely, satisfying your soul.

That summer serving as a valet, my hunger wasn't simply about driving cooler cars. More than that, it was about helping more people. I've always felt a calling to serve. After high school, I got accepted and entered the United States Naval Academy with the clear purpose of serving my family and my country. I wanted greater influence because I wanted to make a greater impact.

Here's what I learned: Achieving more is intentional, not accidental. *Your influence increases in direct proportion to your appetite.*

You Need the Right "Fuel" to Increase Your Impact

So, how do you get a bigger appetite? Obviously, visiting a buffet line isn't the answer. If you want to *be more,* you must regularly consume the Four Fuel Groups.

Fuel One: See More

If you want to *be more,* you have to *see more.*

That summer, I saw *more* than my little apartment complex. I saw *more* than the bills stuffed into my mom's mailbox with my name on it. Instead, I saw myself sitting behind the wheel of a 7 Series BMW, driving down the road of my choosing.

Until that time, I felt like *life* was driving me instead of *me* driving life. When you see yourself disconnected from your potential you feel powerless. Hopelessness sets in. It's the unavoidable byproduct of being subject to your circumstances.

Looking back, I now realize I suffered from a victim mentality. I wasn't a bad person; I was just unaware of my own resourcefulness. When you're living as a victim, you believe the world happens to you. You lose a sense of responsibility for your own life.

Blaming gives you a platform—an audience to voice the injustices and excuses that block your goal. In this state of mind, your unimpressive results aren't your fault—they're someone else's. You find fulfillment in adding to the drama by surrounding yourself with people who agree with the story inside your head.

You initiate conversations that strengthen your version of the truth.

You gather sympathetic listeners who listen to your stories.

You play songs that confirm the injustice.

You watch films that add color and richness to your interpretation of reality.

In this state, the world seems manageable—maybe not ideal, but at least predictable and controllable. While living as a victim, you believe other people or circumstances are to blame for your lack of success, income, and luck.

I think if we're honest, we all live as victims in certain areas.

Do You Know Lady Luck?

In the past, I put way too much stock in things like luck and chance. You grow up believing well-intended people who regift the same warmed over clichés regifted to them years before. Clichés about luck like, *"It's not what you know; it's who you know."* By believing this, you can blame your plateau on people you don't even know.

The truth is, before others choose to believe in you, they naturally judge if you believe in yourself. I know people who emitted the right frequency and drew the right people to them because of it.

Luck had little to do with it.

Do You Leave It Up To Chance?

Maybe you've been told the cliché about chance: *"You need to be at the right place at the right time."* I've never found a map that led to the "right place" and, unfortunately, the voice inside my GPS doesn't know how to find those coordinates either. (I asked it one day back when I was a valet.)

This old cliché draws the illogical conclusion that you somehow stumble into greatness when you stumble into the right space. The truth is, if you're unaware, the right space isn't going to help you anyway. The truth is, if you've prepared for the moment, the moment is prepared for you. In other words, your preparation creates the right time and puts you in the right place. I know people who won while in the wrong place at the wrong time and others who lost when they were in the right place at the right time.

Chance had little to do with it.

Back then, I kept thinking luck and chance would visit me someday. The truth is, I never heard them knock. They may have dropped in on family and friends, but for some reason they skipped my mom's apartment. Who knows? Maybe they forgot I lived there? *I* certainly wished I didn't remember.

I eventually realized focusing on my apartment zip code didn't change my results, no matter how much energy I exerted. Regardless of my distraction tactics, I couldn't change reality by avoiding the truth or by blaming other people or circumstances. So, rather than complaining, that summer I shifted my strategy. I began to feast on the Four Fuel Groups.

Because I wanted to *be more,* I knew I had to *see more.*

Seeing more may mean hanging out with different friends. It might mean watching different television programs or limiting your television intake altogether. It may mean changing your environment or your habits. For me, it meant redesigning my life—what I read, where I went, and who spoke into my life.

It's been said the only difference between being stuck in a rut and stuck in the ground is six feet. You get the point. Slow death occurs when you stay stuck.

So where is STUCK? The better question is, where *isn't* it?

Let's face it, we're creatures of habit who naturally avoid pain. We gravitate toward familiarity and predictability. Anyone can find STUCK very easily—just look for your "comfort zone" and you'll find it close by.

When you live from your comfort zone, you convince yourself you're content—that you're satisfied with satisfactory.

But you're not.

When you're not growing and creating the life you know you're meant to experience, your spirit stirs. You use words to describe the place you are, the place of your discontentment. You conceive of something better, but you're not sure how to get there.

Notice, STUCK doesn't always mean you're unsuccessful. On my Higher Life Design travels, I've met plenty of STUCK successful people. Success creates a unique kind of comfort zone, too. Just ask the safest man in the world. He's easy to find. Just look for the one who has everything to lose. Instead of living life "playing to win," he's settled for living life "playing not to lose."

History proves success is the beginning of obsolescence. Just look at GM, K-Mart, Circuit City, or countless other companies who have already seen their best days. Success signals your eventual downfall if you fail to keep your eyes open. Success makes many individuals and organizations stay safe, comfortable, mediocre, average, and status quo. They simply replicate rather than creatively innovate.

If you want escape the comfort zone and *be more,* you have to *see more.*

Fuel Two: Eat More

If you want to *be more* you have to *eat more.*

That summer, I became insatiably curious. I knew the patrons at the restaurant weren't smarter or better than me. Still, I knew they had found something that had eluded me. They lived in the same country and breathed the same air, but they had achieved completely different results. Perplexed, I started showing an interest and asking questions and after some time, I discovered their secret.

Clearly, they were eating more than me!

In my industry, there's a simple but brilliant phrase often tossed around: *"Your income follows your personal growth."*

The first time I heard it, I had my doubts. "If I invested more money on myself, then I'd make more money?" It almost sounds foolish, unless you understand the science behind it. Let's apply these principles to your home, as an example, and see if it all shakes out.

Imagine investing $30,000 to renovate your outdated kitchen. You do all the work yourself: designing, building, installing, all of it—every square inch. Because this is a fictional illustration, let's also imagine the project turns out brilliantly. (For me, this *would be* the fictional part of the story.) When you eventually put your house on the market, would you include the cost of those renovations in your list price? (It's not a trick question.)

Would your asking price reflect the personal investment you made measured in time, talent, and treasure? Would you be satisfied if the buyer offered you $20,000 less than what you paid—even before the renovation? (Again, it's not a trick question.)

Of course your selling price would be higher. Because you invested more, you'd expect to be paid more.

I saw this personal growth principle reenacted every day. Although I didn't thrive in formal academics, I've always been a healthy fan of income. Unknowingly stuck in my ignorance, I didn't see the connection until that summer.

The high-end restaurant I worked at had a close-knit community. I discovered that despite their success, these customers continued to invest more money on their personal growth. The content they chose differed, but they all experienced the same payoff. Conferences, seminars, books, and coaching—

these customers consumed it all. Their level of personal income followed their level of personal growth.

Today, I'm living proof that this principle works. As I added value to myself, I made myself more valuable.

So many people are waiting for others to bet on them. Sadly, they're unwilling to bet on themselves. Think about it, though. Why would anyone want to invest in them? These people are quick to spend their money on possessions, but they're slow to invest in their own growth. This is a direct reflection of their low self-image.

Here's why.

People don't invest in something unless they see value in it. When people refuse to invest in themselves, they make a loud public announcement about their own self-worth. And if they don't see worth in themselves, why would others want to buy from them? They subconsciously tell others, "Don't buy from me; I don't have anything worth investing in." This self-sabotaging cycle saddens me, but I see it way too often.

When I speak to audiences today, some of them are shocked to discover I regularly invest tens of thousands of dollars in my own personal growth. Last year alone, I invested much more than $100,000. This amount may sound alarming until they realize I made much more than $1,000,000.

It comes down to perspective. If I want to play at a higher level, I need to be around people who are going further and faster than me.

In the following chapters, we'll take a deeper look into the science behind this truth. For now, keep consuming more quality content because if you want to *be more,* you have to *eat more.*

Fuel Three: Decree More

If you want to *be more* you have to *decree more.*

"My family is financially cursed."

I recently heard one of my teammates make this passing comment. I almost jumped out of my seat when I heard her statement.

"What did you just say?" I asked with a keen interest, making sure not to misunderstand her.

Feeling caught, she initially defended her statement. However, after a little coaxing she went on to retell the story inside her head. She told me about her grandparents, how they had struggled to make ends meet. Two amazing people, defined by incredible care and compassion, these elderly people passed on without a dime to their names.

This pattern continued with her own parents. According to her, they did the best they could. She elaborated on their kindness and love, but also emphasized the unwelcome burden of bills and poverty that pursued them her entire childhood. The stress of "not having enough" eventually took its toll.

She finished her story with the same deafening decree, "See, I told you. My family is financially cursed."

I heard her words and then served them right back to her subconscious mind.

"Are you a mother?" I asked with genuine interest.

"Yes," she answered, "of two beautiful children."

"Do you *want* them to be financially cursed?" I continued.

"Of course not," she quickly responded.

"Then, why would you decree this reality upon them?" I challenged.

"What do you mean?"

"I mean, why would you speak this *past* reality into your *future* results? Words are incredibly powerful. Verbal decrees prepare and position us to receive certain results. I believe declarations function like seeds which grow into mature fruit. If you don't *want* that fruit in your *future,* don't *plant* those seeds in your *present.*"

When I finished speaking, I looked at her and saw her eyes brighten. She had hope. It's almost as if she realized she had the power to plant other seeds than the ones planted by her parents and grandparents.

It's not enough to simply remove the bad seeds. You must replace them with better seeds. So, I gave her a different decree from my favorite book.

> "*'For I know the plans I have for you,' declares the Lord, 'plans to prosper you and not to harm you, plans to give you hope and a future.'*"[5]

She began declaring this new decree over herself and her family. Months later, she and her daughters were reaping a new reality. Her good seeds produced an initial harvest much different from the one of her childhood. This subtle shift expanded her awareness. It allowed her to see herself outside the curse that held her potential captive.

When you look up "decree" in the dictionary, you suddenly understand the tremendous weight this word carries.

decree[6]
1. an authoritative order having the force of law
2. the judgment of a court
3. an administrative act applying or interpreting articles of canon law
4. a legally binding command or decision entered on the court record
5. one of the eternal purposes of God, by which events are foreordained

Trust me, I'm not a walking dictionary.

When I heard my teammate *decree* that curse, I had no idea there were five total meanings for the word. I knew the word *decree* had power, but certainly not that much power! Consider this definition the next time you make a *decree*.

You inject authority into your words.

You drive them home and drill them deep.

You implant results by internalizing your reality.

Be Careful What You Argue For

This teammate had made a legally binding agreement with toxic results she didn't even desire. She argued for something she didn't want. Although it might sound illogical, it's something we all do. Here are two examples to illustrate what I mean.

Ask a heroin addict if she wants to be free. Most likely, she'll say, "Yes." Then, when you try to create a plan to help her stop, she'll argue, claiming why it won't work for her.

- "You don't understand; all my friends are heroin addicts, too."
- "You don't understand; I can't make it a day without it."
- "You don't understand; my dealer is my neighbor."
- "You don't understand; I need it."

You've probably heard about the power heroin holds over its users, yet you've also heard how people say they'd give anything to kick the habit. Despite their best intentions, many addicts give up before they even start. They argue for that which they don't want.

Not all of us can relate to heroin, so let's use a more universal example—money.

Imagine your annual income. If you don't know the exact number, just take your best guess. Now, imagine that amount being your monthly income. Would you like that reality?

Most people would enjoy this arrangement. But if you asked them to create a plan to achieve this, most would argue why it's an impossibility.

- "You don't understand; I don't have the necessary degree, training, or skills."
- "You don't understand; my situation is different."

- "You don't understand; I'm from a small town."
- "You don't understand; I can't do that."

Both of these illustrations—the heroin example and the money example—prove a powerful point: *you don't get what you want; you get what you argue for.*

Decrees wield more power than desires. *What you say (decree) about yourself* packs more punch than *what you say you want (desire).* You must make a legal agreement with the future life you want, not the present life you have in order to achieve it.

Simply put, to *be more,* you must *decree more.*

Fuel Four: Free More

If you want to *be more,* you have to *free more.*

"I feel so overwhelmed. I just wish there were more hours in a day."

Have you ever *heard* those words?

Have you ever *said* those words?

Chances are you've at least *felt* this way.

However, this logic wouldn't fix your problems. If you had more hours in your day, you'd simply fill it with more activity. You'd never accomplish all your important goals. The problem isn't lack of time; it's lack of *decision.*

You might think I'm going to tell you to stop spending time surfing the Internet, watching television, and reading magazines. Breathe easy. I'm not. That's secondary. What I'm referring to is primary.

See, those activities aren't the main problem. They simply explain how you intentionally distract yourself from the real issues pulling at your awareness.

If I could spend a week following most people, I'd observe them spending buckets of time on unnecessary topics, relationships, activities, and thoughts. This tendency simply clutters your creativity and holds you hostage from your Higher Life Design. Although most of us have undesirable clutter in our lives, we tolerate it because we don't enjoy the alternative—KILLING things!

Exploring the definition of decide helps explain what I mean by "killing." The English word *decide* comes from the Latin word *decidere,* meaning "to cut off." Its cousin, the related Latin word *caedere,* means "to cut" or "to kill."[7]

Think of all the English words similar to *decide*. Here are a few:

- homicide
- insecticide
- genocide
- pesticide
- suicide

These words all come from the same Latin word: *caedere.* So, when you make a decision, you're literally "killing your options." You're cutting off other possibilities and freeing up extra mental space. Deciding is the Mr. Clean of mental clutter.

So, why don't we rush to make decisions? Do we despise Mr. Clean?

Not at all.

In a strange way, whenever you make a decision, you experience a type of loss. Avoiding decisions prevents you from feeling loss. However, what you fail to realize in doing so is that *not* making a decision is actually a decision. You'll never be confronted with the exact same opportunity in the exact moment ever again. By choosing *not* to decide, you're actually *deciding* to stay exactly where you are.

Dan Ariely, author of *Predictably Irrational,* explains the psychology behind indecision. "Closing a door on an option is experienced as a loss, and people are willing to pay a price to avoid the emotion of a loss."[8] There's a cost in deciding, but there's also a cost in *not* deciding.

That summer as a valet, I realized a powerful principle: successful people make quicker decisions and rarely go back on them. Unsuccessful people make slower decisions and often go back on them.

Steer Clear of the Mental Traffic Jam

Remember those people who regifted you myths about luck and chance? Unfortunately, they also regifted you something else that slows you down. They taught you to keep your options open. The tendency is to let many decisions go undecided. We rationalize putting them off until we get more information, more resources, or more clarity.

The truth is, most of the time we put them off indefinitely. We don't really want to make the decision anyway, so we wait for circumstances, people, or life to decide for us.

This logic only feeds mediocrity and apathy.

Listen to any guru and you'll hear one common theme about activity: *it's impossible to do many things well.* When you put off decisions, you give those unaddressed issues permission to take up mental space. (For tech people, think of mental RAM.)

By trying to focus on too much, you deny the truth that you have a limited amount of brain space. Filling up active memory with dozens of unmade decisions clogs up your conscious and unconscious mind. It bars your positive creativity.

This mental traffic jam manifests itself in self-limiting statements.

"I feel overwhelmed."

"I'm drained."

"I need caffeine."

"I can't concentrate."

"I'm running on fumes."

"I'm too stressed to function."

These common phrases are like check engine lights alerting us to internal performance issues. To increase your output, you need to decrease the demands on your mental RAM. This only happens when you free up space by making decisions.

In his book, *Discover Your Sweet Spot,* Scott M. Fay explains this principle. "Until we get comfortable killing off a current activity, we'll never be able to start a new one effectively. By killing off the old, we find the needed space for something new; something we should start doing."⁹

Kill first. Fill second.

What decisions have you been avoiding?

How long have you been avoiding them?

How much mental space would you free up by making a decision?

Although decisions might involve pain, avoiding them only prolongs the pain. Pain is inevitable, but misery is a choice.

To *be more,* you must *free more*—mental RAM included.

Get Ready to Pack

Our trip is far from over. Truly, we've only just started. We're still in the TAKEOFF phase with many choices ahead. In the next chapter, we'll explore how Higher Life Design Travelers should pack.

In my transition from valet to international marketer, I almost packed the wrong bags. Doing so would have sabotaged my flight on the Higher Life Design. I would have been grounded before I was even airborne.

Like you, I have the right to bring whatever baggage I want. But remember, improper packing costs way more in the end. I've learned this firsthand.

To help with the packing process, I now use a checklist. So, at the end of each chapter, we'll include part of the Higher Life Design Traveler's Checklist. Today, when working with my team of more than 100,000 leaders, I've found checklists help drive principles deeper.

Because you're hungry for more, I think you'll find it useful.

Higher Life Design Traveler's Checklist

- ☐ I realize apathy isn't an option and plateauing isn't acceptable.
- ☐ I take responsibility for my life so I can move myself in a new direction.
- ☐ I invest proper time and energy into exploring the marketplace so my hunger for more increases.
- ☐ I examine the best practices and the most effective methods for my destination.
- ☐ I take proper action so I don't become a spectator in my own life.
- ☐ I prepare for the moment so the moment is prepared for me.
- ☐ I "see more" by getting out of my comfort zone.
- ☐ I "eat more" by consuming content that helps me grow.
- ☐ I "decree more" by planting only good seeds about my future so my past no longer holds me back.
- ☐ I "free up more" mental space (RAM) by making overdue decisions so I can go further faster.

Step Two: Pack Your Bags

*The right packing eliminates
the wrong baggage*

When I met Jefferson, I had hit a plateau in my professional career. Although I had quite a bit of success in the past, I realized there were some things still holding me back. After working with him, I was able to identify what was holding me back from my past and change this way of thinking. I also broke through new barriers by learning strategies for clear goal setting. Today you'll find me consistently creating my Higher Life Design.

— **April C.**

Jefferson is a true leader who has a passion to see people win. As an entrepreneur, I've had several setbacks and found myself stuck in the past. Jefferson helped me understand not to compare myself to others. Through his own life, he demonstrates it's not where you start but rather where you finish. Thanks, Jefferson, for helping me throw out the past and focus on a bigger, more amazing future. I'm keeping my eyes on the prize and Designing a Higher Life.

— **Max K.**

Befor you board the Higher Life Design flight, you must evaluate your inventory and consider your carry-ons.

Let's be honest—most of us have held on far too long to unnecessary bags that only create unnecessary baggage in our lives. Toxic relationships, unprofitable habits, poisonous grudges, bitter jealousies, unchecked addictions, and unhealthful unforgiveness only add weight to the journey. To arrive at your intended destination healthy, wealthy, and happy, you must exert discernment and discipline within the packing process.

Bags don't fly free. Each carries a cost. Some are worth the trip and others should stay grounded. *The right packing eliminates the wrong baggage.*

Novices simply stuff their suitcases without much thought. Their casual intentions end up costing them in the long run. Every unnecessary item adds extra weight and extra effort.

Higher Life Design Travelers pack with the end in mind. They understand the difference between baggage and luggage. One you don't want. The other you do.

Baggage hinders you on your journey.

baggage
1. intangible things (such as feelings, circumstances, or beliefs) that get in the way[10]
2. burdensome practices, regulations, ideas, or traits
3. things that encumber one's freedom; impediments[11]

Luggage helps you on your journey.

luggage
1. personal belongings for a journey[12]

Here's why you *don't* want baggage:

Baggage Costs More Than You Imagine

Baggage sabotages your success. It weighs you down and creates space between you and your ultimate goal. Many times you carry it unknowingly. I certainly did. Back in my apartment days, I let many thoughts and behaviors hold me back.

I explain this phenomenon with the acronym B.A.G.G.A.G.E. Check out the meaning and then take a look at your own life. Are you carrying any baggage with you?

B. = Blame
A. = Arrogance
G. = Greed
G. = Grudges
A. = Apathy
G. = Grumbling
E. = Envy

B = Blame

Blaming places responsibility on other people and circumstances. By blaming, you abdicate your power and announce your ignorance. Instead of happening to the world, you see the world as something that happens to you. You react rather than respond.

This low level of awareness begins in infancy. Little children blame poor choices on others.

"He made me do it."

"She hit me first."

"It's all your fault."

Because most children see themselves as victims, blaming comes naturally. Refusing to take responsibility lets them off the hook and prevents them from making changes. Although we all start here as kids, many people stay here—for decades!

We may chuckle when a six-year-old blames his missing homework on the dog who thought it was a meal. However, when a 36-year-old adult blames his incomplete project on a failed computer backup, it's not so funny.

Higher Life Design Travelers refuse to pack blame with them on their journey.

A = Arrogance

It's nearly impossible to teach arrogant people something new. *They already "know" everything.* A quick google search of "arrogant athletes" produces some interesting results. Serena Williams may show up on a list or two, but for the most part, males pridefully gobble up the top spots.

My favorite book warns, "Pride comes before the fall."[13] Yet arrogant athletes reject such wisdom. Without surprise, many of them experience moral failure at some time in their lives.

Of course, nobody wants to follow an insecure or fearful leader and, for this reason, Higher Life Design Travelers pack a high level of self-confidence with them. However, there's a fine line between confidence and arrogance.

Dr. Alan Goldberg knows the difference between the two. He served as a sports psychology consultant to the 1999 NCAA men's basketball national champions and the 2000 NCAA men's soccer national champions.

Dr. Goldberg said, "Most great athletes do think that they are THE BEST! This kind of inner self-confidence is actually essential to your ultimate success within your sport. What isn't essential to your success however is telling everyone else that you're the best! What is downright ugly and tasteless is going around acting out this internal attitude…. Acting entitled, cocky, and like you're God's gift to creation will alienate those around you, make you look like you're a lousy sport, and will ultimately set you up to fail."[14]

Former UFC champion Anderson Silva felt the sting of arrogance on July 6, 2013. Known for his unnecessary taunts, UFC 162 proved no exception, but this time his arrogance wounded him—and his record—permanently.

Silva had reason to be confident. The former champion reigned the UFC middleweight division for nearly seven years. Over time, his 17-fight win streak slowly shifted into arrogance.

On that summer night, in classic Silva style, he talked, taunted, and dared challenger Chris Weidman to engage him. "Yet when the champion lowered his hands early in the second round, Weidman caught him with a short left that sent the MMA star to the mat. Weidman pounced and landed a few more shots that forced the referee to stop the fight."[15]

Weidman sent a shock wave through mixed martial arts as he became the new middleweight champion.

Arrogance delivered Silva a near knockout that night. If he humbles himself, he could recover, rebuild, and return. If he continues to fight with arrogance, another knockout is inevitable.

Although not perfect, Higher Life Design Travelers refuse to pack arrogance with them on their journey. They only allow room for confidence.

G = Greed

Motivational speaker Zig Ziglar said, "Money is not everything but it ranks right up there with oxygen."[16] It sounds humorous, but in some ways he has a point. In this life, we need resources to sustain life.

Higher Life Design Travelers keep money in its proper place. They recognize money is simply a tool, nothing more, nothing less. It can't bring people back from the dead or add years to your life. It can't erase bad memories or create joy. Money merely provides options.

Healthy people *use* money and *love* people. Unhealthy people *love* money and *use* people. Baggage comes when money becomes our motivation.

I enjoy money and I've used the Higher Life Design to create an incredible life. I love taking trips all over the world with my family. We visit exotic places with amazing friends. I've felt the rush of flying in a helicopter with my wife, Megan, off the coast of Monaco. I've seen the beauty of the Yucatán Peninsula while zip lining above the treetops.

Along with our extensive international travel, I enjoy being at home, too. We recently installed an amazing backyard pool complete with waterfall features, an outdoor kitchen, hot tub, and a fire pit. We love relaxing in this paradise lagoon outlined with rustic boulders and flagstone.

Although it takes money to live, make no mistake just *having money* isn't living. Plenty of people stockpile resources without thinking about how to use those resources. Greed is a feeling you don't want to carry with you. It's an excessive desire to acquire more than you need or deserve.

One of my favorite authors, John C. Maxwell, is an incredibly generous man who provides a proper perspective about resources. "God loves to give to you what he knows will flow through you." Maxwell encourages us to be a river, not a reservoir. When we cut off generosity, we simultaneously invite greediness. By failing to give, we fail to grow.

Higher Life Design Travelers feel lighter than most because they share their resources with others. I've designed my life around a company designed to give back to others. We're dedicated to making a difference in the world.[17]

Through our own charitable organization and other key partner organizations worldwide, we help support worthwhile causes that promote clean water, cross-cultural understanding, and entrepreneurship in developing nations.

We do more than just write checks. We've pioneered a movement called "VolunTourism"—group vacations with a social purpose. For years, we've planned and participated in numerous VolunTourism trips to remote locations in Africa, Latin America, and Asia, helping the most vulnerable people among us: children.

Higher Life Design Travelers refuse to pack greed with them on their journey.

G = Grudges

One of the easiest ways to weigh yourself down is by carrying a grudge. John Lennon wisely warned, "Holding on to anger, resentment, and hurt only gives you tense muscles. Forgiveness gives you back the lightness in your life."[18]

Several times in my own journey I could have let grudges dominate my thinking. Like most people, I experienced broken relationships and betrayal. Quite easily, this could have become my focus. When we don't have much going for us, we can cling to this pain as an excuse not to move forward.

Many times you have the right to be angry. You were offended, mistreated, or slighted. However, when you let bitterness and grudges fill your mental space, you're the one who suffers most. Many times perpetrators move on mentally, while their victims feel fresh wounds on a daily basis for decades to come.

As much as you want to be free, a grudge indicates what psychologists call a trauma bond.[19] Author Catherine Ponder explains, "When you hold resentment, you are bound to that person or condition by an emotional link that is stronger than steel. Forgiveness is the only way to dissolve that link and get free."[20]

Author Lewis B. Smedes exhorts, "To forgive is to set a prisoner free and discover that the prisoner was you."[21] Although forgiving doesn't mean forgetting, it's a choice you make independent of the way you feel.

No one knew this better than Ravensbrück concentration camp survivor Corrie ten Boom. She and her sister, Betsie, were arrested for concealing Jews in their home during the Nazi occupation of Holland. Betsie died in the camp. Corrie survived.

ten Boom remembered a time years after the war when she encountered a former Nazi guard in a public place. Evidently, this guard knew of her prior imprisonment. Feeling remorse for his actions, he offered an apology. He stood before her and extended his hand hoping she would reciprocate. She had a choice. Would she extend forgiveness, or would she carry a grudge?

At that particular moment, she certainly didn't feel like forgiving. Later, she reflected upon the truth about the situation.

"Since the end of the war, I had had a home in Holland for victims of Nazi brutality. Those who were able to forgive their former enemies were able also to return to the outside world and rebuild their lives, no matter what the physical scars. Those who nursed their bitterness remained invalids. It was as simple and as horrible as that."[22]

Knowing the cost of not forgiving, ten Boom decided to forgive and release her grudge. Her words to the guard reflected the release she felt only *after* she made the mental decision.

"'I forgive you, brother!' I cried. 'With all my heart!'

"For a long moment we grasped each other's hands, the former guard and the former prisoner. I had never known God's love so intensely, as I did then.'"[23]

ten Boom discovered the secret of traveling light. It begins with forgiveness. If you fail to forgive, life is governed by an endless cycle of resentment and retaliation.[24]

Higher Life Design Travelers refuse to pack grudges with them on their journey.

A = *Apathy*

Millennials (people born from the early 1980s to the early 2000s) unfortunately often get a bad rap. [25] Experts critique and compare them to previous generations. They've been labeled "The Lost Generation" by some and "The Apathetic Generation" by others.

However, there are exceptions to the stereotypes. The ones breaking the mold—among the Millennials or any other generation—aren't lost or apathetic. They know who they are and why they're here. They carry luggage, not baggage.

They're different because they've discovered their why, their way, their will, and their wings. Here's what this clarity means:

What They've Discovered	What This Means
Their "Why"	They have a purpose.
Their "Way"	They have a path.
Their "Will"	They have discipline.
Their "Wings"	They have courage.

Higher Life Design Travelers don't need external motivation. Instead, they merely tap into their internal inspiration. Their strong sense of "why" enables them to discover a plethora of "hows." Rather than finding excuses, their creativity helps them discover solutions. These paths are the "way" they live out their "why." Because it is purpose-driven, apathy is shut out and they maintain discipline—their "will." Finally, when the going gets tough—and it always gets tough—they have the courage to keep moving toward their "why"—courage lifts the spirit, becoming their "wings" in flight.

Whereas apathetic people *wait* for life to happen to them. Higher Life Design Travelers *make* life happen. They refuse to pack apathy with them on their journey.

G = Grumbling

You've probably heard people say:

- "This place gives me the creeps."
- "I sense someone staring at me."
- "That guy gives me a bad vibe."
- "I feel at peace when I go there."

Each of these comments reflect a powerful principle—frequency.

Every living being around you gives off a frequency. This is why you're attracted to some people and repelled by others. Your frequency and theirs either resonate in harmony or clash in dissonance. It's also the reason some places create a sense of calm and others provide a feeling of unrest.

Like most principles, this one can be misapplied or taken out of context. Yet, when you work with this principle, you can make it work for you rather than against you.

Although you can't control what people think of you, you can control the way you present yourself, including your attitude.

Grumbling emits an incredibly negative frequency that repels people. Walk into a public place where someone's grumbling and you'll observe a common scenario. The negative frequency dominates the entire atmosphere. People feel embarrassed for the person grumbling. They avoid eye contact, attempting to sidestep the awkwardness.

Take a quick scan at some of the synonyms for grumble:

> bellyache, bleat, croak, fuss, gripe, grizzle, grouch, growl, complain, grump, moan, murmur, mutter, nag, repine, scream, squawk, squeal, wail, whimper, whine, yammer[26]

Read these words, then tell me how you feel. I'm guessing you don't feel "up" or optimistic.

Studies show that increased exposure to grumbling creates unhealthful levels of the hormone cortisol. Known as "the stress hormone," this substance is secreted into the bloodstream during times of stress.[27] Small amounts experienced in fight or flight scenarios provide powerful benefits, including:

- a quick burst of energy for survival reasons,
- heightened memory functions,
- a burst of increased immunity, and
- a decreased sensitivity to pain.

However, higher levels of cortisol and prolonged exposure can be hazardous to your health. It produces several negative effects, including:

- impaired cognitive performance,
- suppressed thyroid function,
- blood sugar imbalances such as hyperglycemia,
- decreased bone density,
- decrease in muscle tissue,
- higher blood pressure,
- lowered immunity and inflammatory responses in the body,
- slowed wound healing, and
- increased abdominal fat.

Some of the health problems associated with increased stomach fat include heart attacks, strokes, developing metabolic syndrome, higher levels of "bad" cholesterol (LDL), and lower levels of "good" cholesterol (HDL)—a condition that may lead to other health problems!

Right now you're emitting a frequency and it's your choice whether it's positive or negative. Your frequency projects much further than you imagine. Because of this, Higher Life Design Travelers refuse to pack grumbling with them on their journey.

E = Envy

Wishing you were somebody else kind of defeats the purpose of God creating you. Envy turns your mindset from abundance (one of the highest frequencies) to scarcity (one of the lowest frequencies). With scarcity, you begin taking inventory of what you lack, rather than what you already have.[28] You consume rather than contribute.

Notice the difference between the two.

Abundance	*Scarcity*
Always More	Never Enough
Share Resources	Hoard Resources
Trusts Easily	Suspects Easily
Invites Competition	Despises Competition
Over Delivers	Under Performs
Optimistic Attitude	Pessimistic Attitude
Big Thinker	Small Thinker
Appreciates Others	Criticizes Others
Embraces Risk	Avoids Risk
Celebrates People	Envies People

Envy poisons you and your potential. It's a toxic "feeling of discontent and resentment aroused by a desire for the possessions or qualities of another."[29] Envy shifts your focus to other people's possessions, position, and persona. This deadly emotion prevents you from improving your own life because you're too focused on someone else's.

Ralph Waldo Emerson said, "Where your attention goes your energy flows."[30] Translation: don't waste your best energy focused on other people's accomplishments. Doing so only sabotages your own.

Social media doesn't help. If you're not careful, the object of your envy can now be transmitted through phones, computers, and tablets every minute of every day.

The only way to eliminate this type of B.A.G.G.A.G.E. is by packing L.U.G.G.A.G.E. instead.

Luggage is what you *do* want, because:

Luggage Pays Incredible Dividends

Unlike baggage, luggage packs success along with it. Luggage equips you and closes the gap between you and your ultimate goal. Although we tend to carry baggage accidentally, luggage is only carried intentionally.

Luggage propels you forward through productive thoughts and behaviors. I explain this phenomenon with the acronym L.U.G.G.A.G.E. Check out the meaning and then take personal inventory to see what you're carrying.

> L. = Loving
> U. = Unleashed
> G. = Gutsy
> G. = Generous
> A. = Active
> G. = Growing
> E. = Enthusiastic

L = Loving

Higher Life Design Travelers pack a lot of love with them on their journey.

One of my mentors, Brendon Burchard, explains the importance and value of love through his own brush with death. According to *Forbes* magazine, "Brendon's story is a compelling one—of narrowly surviving a car accident at age 19 on a dark and steamy Caribbean night, and standing, bleeding, atop the crumpled hood of his wrecked car faced with the concept of mortality. In that one moment between life and death, he discovered that at the end of our lives we will all ask, 'Did I live? Did I love? Did I matter?'"[31]

After spending a significant amount of time with this 8-figure earner, I can genuinely say Brendon lives his message of love. He integrates this passion into his work and life. For Brendon, it starts with self-love and then radiates outward. His message is so strong, people actually feel it, as reported by *Forbes* contributor Kathy Caprino. "There's something about Brendon when you speak with him—he 'vibrates' at a level that's different from others, and it feels to me like he has messages we all need to hear but most of us resist."

Although love is an important message, it's often one of the most commonly *misunderstood* messages. Some of the confusion comes from the way we use the word. "Love" can have multiple meanings in multiple contexts. For example, I'll say statements like:

- "I love college football."
- "I love airplanes."
- "I love my wife and son."

Obviously, I love my wife and son much more than college football.

But besides multiple meanings, there are also multiple types of love. Understanding the difference between conditional love and unconditional love helps clear up the confusion.

conditional love

This type of love is "earned" based on conscious or unconscious conditions being met by the lover. In this relationship, the parties must perform a certain set of stated or unstated actions or attitudes to maintain the love. If the parties fail to fulfill obligations, love is withheld or removed from the relationship.

unconditional love

This type of love is freely given regardless of performance or behavior. In this relationship, the parties aren't required to perform a certain set of stated or unstated actions or attitudes to maintain the love. Even if the parties fail to fulfill expectations, love is not withheld or removed from the relationship.

Higher Life Design Travelers express and embody unconditional love in their relationships.

A few years ago, a variety of authors, artists, designers, and musicians created content hoping to shift the way we perceive love from a feeling to an action. The unofficial movement many called "Love is a Verb" helped dispel myths.[32] True love must surpass emotions and express itself through action. Avoid packing any other type.

U = Unleashed

Higher Life Design Travelers choose to be real. It's the only way they know how to fly. These unleashed individuals are incredibly refreshing because they're so rare. In fact, the majority of people aren't unleashed. According to experts, 70% of people struggle with the Impostor Syndrome.[33] They feel they don't know themselves. They feel like they're phonies and frauds. They describe their fears with phrases like:

- "I'm a fake."
- "I'm going to be found out."
- "*They* made a mistake and I shouldn't be here."

Put another way, sufferers of this syndrome believe a discrepancy exists between how they see themselves and how others see them. Although other people might see them one way on the outside, they hardly feel that way on the inside. Fixating on this gap, they feel like phonies and frauds, believing it's only a matter of time until their cover is blown and the world finds out what they already know to be true—they are imposters.

Actors aren't immune. In a *Toronto Star* article titled "The Imposter Syndrome: Behind the Mask," celebrities including Mike Myers, Kate Winslet, Michelle Pfeiffer, and Jodie Foster admitted feeling like imposters—like they're only a breath away from being found out by the "talent police."[34]

In an interview with Mike Wallace of *60 Minutes*, Foster explained that upon notification of winning the Academy Award for best actress she thought it was a fluke. "The same way [I did] when I walked on the campus at Yale. I thought everybody would find out and they'd take the Oscar back. They'd come to my house, knocking on the door; 'Excuse me, we meant to give that to someone else. That was going to Meryl Streep.'"[35]

As long as you focus on feelings of inadequacy, it's impossible to live an unleashed life. Of course we all feel inadequate at times, but the difference with Higher Life Design Travelers is that they transcend these feelings. They address their accusers and deal with their demons. This courage enables them to be the best versions of themselves—the true, unleashed version. When they're unleashed, they're both free and powerful.

G = Gutsy

Plato is thought to have said, "Be kind, for everyone you meet is fighting a hard battle."[36]

Higher Life Design Travelers recognize this battle and run toward it rather than away from it. These Travelers play to *win*, while most others simply play *not to lose*. There's a big difference.

The majority of people are risk averse. They see the potential for failure and respond by insulating and isolating. They settle for playing safe and playing small. In movie vernacular, they're the ones distracted by "the Matrix" and comfortable in "The Shire." [37]

Gutsy people are the opposite. They're bold, determined, and courageous.[38] Hardly reckless, these Travelers not only understand the potential risk, but also the potential reward. This gap creates fuel, not fear.

This type of gutsy living inspires stories, movies, and legends. It's captured in blockbusters like *Braveheart* and lesser known dramas like *Freedom Fighters*. In these films and stories, the hero saw challenges and chose to engage despite popular opinion.

Here are the plot summaries:

Braveheart
Hero: Sir William Wallace

This Academy Award winning film from 1995 is based on the historical true story of a Scottish landowner who became one of the main leaders during the Wars of Scottish Independence. Wallace (portrayed by Mel Gibson) was captured in Robroyston, near Glasgow, and handed over to King Edward I of England. King Edward had Wallace hanged, drawn, and quartered for alleged high treason and crimes against English civilians.

Following his death, Wallace obtained an iconic status far beyond his homeland. He is the protagonist of the fifteenth century epic poem "The Acts and Deeds of Sir William Wallace, Noble of Elderslie." Wallace is also the subject of literary works by Sir Walter Scott and Jane Porter.[39]

Freedom Writers
Hero: Erin Gruwell

Based on the book *The Freedom Writers Diaries* by teacher Erin Gruwell, this film tells the story of more than 100 teens at Woodrow Wilson Classical High School in Eastside, Long Beach, California, who used writing to change themselves and the world around them.

These students had been written off by everyone around them and people scoffed at her chances of succeeding with them. Regardless, Gruwell (portrayed by Hilary Swank) wasn't about to let them go down without a fight. She used the writings of Anne Frank *(The Diary of a Young Girl)* and Zlata Filipović *(Zlata's Diary: A Child's Life in Wartime Sarajevo)* to engage her students with the English language and more importantly, teach them compassion and acceptance in difficult circumstances like their own. This gave the students hope and a belief they could overcome their circumstances because they were not alone in their struggles.[40]

While most stood by, afraid to act, Wallace and Gruwell embraced the risk and acted. Their small chance of victory motivated them to risk defeat. They bet on themselves and their ability to inspire those around them. Although the cost proved high, their gutsy actions created their legacies and changed lives.

Higher Life Design Travelers pack plenty of guts with them on their journey.

G = Generous

I met Wayne Nugent in 1997 when I was a junior at Texas Christian University. My friend, James, had a girlfriend who knew Wayne's girlfriend. A few years older than us, in many ways Wayne was someone we wanted to emulate. A millionaire at the age of 28, his results differed from the valet life I knew. Even then, I knew Wayne seemed destined for greatness. Although most people wait for luck or chance to show up, Wayne hunted down success with animal-like instincts. During the next few years, he became a high-level performer, building several organizations to more than 100,000 sales reps and $100 million in sales.

I benefitted from Wayne's generosity both directly and indirectly. He helped me think differently by helping me think bigger. He introduced incredible resources to me like books, beliefs, and behaviors.

Books

Wayne taught me that to be a leader, I needed to become a reader. Back as a valet, I didn't see the connection between personal growth and income. As author James Allen described, "I was anxious to improve my circumstances, but unwilling to improve myself; therefore, I remained bound."[41]

Books became one of the keys that helped me transition from poverty to prosperity. I'm incredibly grateful to many of these "mentors" I never met. Although some of these authors died decades ago, I'm indebted to the legacy they left through the lessons captured in their words.

Slowly, I was beginning to change. My self-image evolved and, for the first time, I saw myself as someone worthy of investment. As I added value to myself, I became more valuable.

Beliefs

When I started, I didn't understand how to build a business. My results proved that. I thought it was about me winning. In the beginning, I focused more on the paycheck and less on the people. I passed out flyers and expected them to do the work for me. As you might have guessed, I didn't make a dime.

Wayne showed me how true success comes by helping others win. Although I started as a solopreneur, I quickly discovered wealth building is a team sport. Wayne challenged my mind and my motives. His generous mentoring slowly shifted my beliefs.

While reflecting upon my college football days, I realized star athletes might attract the hype, but only teams celebrate long-term success when they work together as one. Sustained wins are the result of strong camaraderie and strong collaboration.

Behaviors

Wayne didn't have to invest in me. Initially, I was an unaware young kid blessed with buckets of ambition. Although ignorant, I knew one thing. If I wanted Wayne to keep on pouring into me I needed to return the favor. I needed to add value in his life.

So that's what I did. I changed my behavior. I served Wayne by putting prospects in front of him. I took Zig Ziglar's advice seriously. I helped Wayne get what he wanted and in the end he helped me get what I wanted.

I took what little money I had and reinvested it in my own growth. One time, I put off getting badly needed new tires in order to attend a training instead. I wanted to be better in business. Although I settled for driving on side roads to avoid a blow out, I realized my sacrifice put me squarely on the road to success.

As Wayne's example proved Higher Life Design Travelers pack plenty of generosity with them on their journey.

A = Active

Life is too short to settle for sedentary living. Higher Life Design Travelers stay active and in control of their physical health. Because your call to serve is great, your call for self-care needs to be just as great. A *big heart* filled with love can't go the distance if it's also a *bad heart* clogged with cholesterol.

According to Dr. James Rouse, one issue hinders people from being their best self. People tend to keep health and wellness in isolation from other parts of their lives. They fail to integrate health because they fail to keep it front and center.[42]

Logically, when you make health your focus, it literally steps up your game in every other area. You lead stronger. You laugh harder. You love longer. And health is holistic, too. Physical health encourages mental health, emotional health, and spiritual health.

I realized long ago my health and fitness are simply an extension of me. I can talk all I want about self-leadership, discipline, and results, but if I fail to embody these lessons in my life, my words don't carry weight. When I carry excessive weight with my body, I fail to carry impressive impact with my words.

My message and motivation mean more when my words and actions match. The audio needs to match the video. Because of this, I've created a simple strategy to keep me grounded. I call it The Act Up System.

The Act Up System
1. Think Up
2. Get Up
3. Give Up
4. Fill Up
5. Rest Up

Let's explore these steps, one at a time.

1. Think Up: *More Reasons*

Don't start listing your "hows" if you haven't first found your "whys." German philosopher Friedrich Nietzsche observed, "He who has a why to live can bear almost any how."[43]

Before you can change your actions you must first choose a correct attitude. Start by writing out all the reasons why health and wellness will help you. A few examples of "whys" include:

- because I want to go up a flight of stairs without running out of breath
- because I want to walk my daughter down the aisle
- because I want to play with my grandchildren
- because I want to feel more confident
- because I want to attend my reunion

Regardless of your answers, you need to get clarity around the reasons "why." A big "why" produces a big chance for victory.

2. Get Up: *More Movement*

Modern life requires less movement. Until a century ago, you probably wouldn't survive unless you moved. In agrarian societies, movement meant eating. In industrial societies, movement meant getting paid. Today, with home offices, escalators, elevators, and public transportation, movement is almost optional.

To reclaim your health, you need to move often and every action counts. I suggest taking breaks every 45–60 minutes. Get up and walk. At a minimum, stand up and stretch. Your body and your brain will reset. Spending hours staring at a screen doesn't help your focus or your health. (In fact, it hurts it!) You may even want to consider transitioning to a standing work station instead of sitting all day.

Commit to a regular exercise routine. I suggest three to five times per week. Everyone is different, so find a level that is comfortable but still challenging to you. Currently, I frequent a local CrossFit facility near my house. Sure, it's intense, but it gives me an edge that goes with me throughout the day.

Decades ago, many fitness gurus targeted "peak performance" as the goal. However, nature teaches us that *what goes up must come down*. Peak performance isn't a sustainable state and opinions have shifted.

Today, the goal is "high performance." Through intentional effort, maintaining this type of sustained, heightened level of energy is possible. I've found two 1-hour cardio routines per week opens my lungs and builds stamina. I also integrate a couple strength-based routines to keep me strong and flexible.

3. Give Up: *More Discipline*

Health and wellness isn't simply about what you consume, it's also about what you *avoid*. Your body needs the proper fuel to function effectively. Higher Life Design Travelers exert discipline by refraining from empty calories and carbohydrate crashes. While this isn't a diet book, some pitfalls to avoid include:

- unhealthful unnatural sweets,
- sugary drinks, alcohol, and excessive caffeine (I prefer green tea instead),
- processed foods and packaged food products,
- starches (white potatoes, potato chips, pastas, etc.), and other high carbohydrate foods, and
- the "three whites": white salt (use unrefined or Celtic sea salt instead), white sugar, and white flour (breads; especially white bread, croissants, and muffins).

Certain diets spike in popularity overnight, such as The Baby Food Diet made popular by celebrity trainer Tracy Anderson.[44] Other approaches build slowly over time, such as the Primal lifestyle by Mark Sisson and the similar paleo diet championed by Dr. Loren Cordain, amongst others.[45]

Regardless of your ultimate food choices, make sure you do adequate research. Examine the results, not just the hype. Remember, you can always try one approach for a month or a few months, see how you feel, and then decide to stay with it, tweak it, or try something else.

Once you identify what to avoid, Act Up by giving up. Your discipline is worth it. Jim Rohn said it best, "We must all suffer from one of two pains: the pain of discipline or the pain of regret. The difference is discipline weighs ounces while regret weighs tons."[46]

4. Fill Up: *More Intelligence*
In some cases, too much of a good thing can be a *good* thing. Act Up by choosing water and the right kinds of food.

Water

The average adult human body is about 60 percent water.[47] Just one percent dehydration will impair your physical and mental capabilities. For this reason, many experts advise drinking five to seven liters of water daily (assuming you are active).

Food

Although conventional wisdom suggested eating three meals a day, some new research suggests four to five small meals is better.[48] "Proponents of this idea claim that eating small meals throughout the day can lower cholesterol, promote weight loss, improve energy levels, boost metabolism, and preserve lean muscle mass." Again, it's important to find what works best for you.

5. Rest Up: *More Sleep*

Before electricity, most people slept 10 hours a night.[49] Blame it on a lack of options, but the pre-electric age people might have been smarter then we think. According to Dr. James B. Maas, quoted in *The New York Times,* "Ten hours a night is a duration we've just recently discovered is ideal for optimal performance. When activity no longer was limited by the day's natural light, sleep habits changed."[50]

Today, remote controls don't help the problem. Our average amount of sleep slipped to eight hours a night. More than one-third of adults now sleep fewer than six hours a night.[51] Dr. Mass explains, "In just the last twenty years we've added 158 hours to our annual working and commuting time—the equivalent of a full month of working hours." Clearly, we're working more and sleeping less.

Although this pace might seem beneficial on the surface, the long-term effects are far reaching. Each year, more people suffer from sleep disorders, accidents related to sleep deprivation, and lost productivity. Experts estimate this cost in hundreds of billions of dollars, not to mention loss of life.

I suggest sleeping 8-9 hours per night. If you miss that target, nap during the day to catch up. Convincing yourself you can be more productive on less sleep is only ignorant. Rest up and see how quickly your quality of life increases.

G = Growing

I'm amazed every time I look at my son, Harrison. I'm not exaggerating when I say he grows overnight. Because he's a toddler, I see him change daily. He's finding his voice and his legs. Sure, he'll fall occasionally, but unlike us adults, he's not afraid of failure. Kids advance rapidly because they're willing to experiment. Looking foolish isn't even on their radar.

Have you ever noticed babies don't blush? They have very little self-awareness. If they're hungry, they cry. If they need to pee, they pee. If they want to chew on the remote—you got it—they chew on the remote. They advance by trial and error. But as we adults progress in life, we tend to regress in risk. We adopt a mindset that it's no longer acceptable to fail or make an error. We settle for a routine where we're in control and everything is familiar.

Eric Hoffer warned us about the cost of not changing: "In times of change, learners inherit the earth; while the learned find themselves beautifully equipped to deal with a world that no longer exists."[52]

Higher Life Design Travelers are the exception. We aren't afraid of change because we know change and growth go hand in hand. We only grow when we're stretched beyond our comfort zones.

Giving up control requires a death of sorts. French writer Anatole France said, "All changes, even the most longed for, have their melancholy; for what we leave behind is part of ourselves; we must die to one life before we can enter into another."[53]

No wonder change is scary. To change is to die and then be reborn. This cycle certainly produces growth, but it also produces inevitable Pain. I experience this every time I get a cell phone upgrade. For the first few days, I hate my new phone. Even though I know the new technology will help me go further faster, I can't stand the learning curve. But after three days, I love the new phone and never want to go back—until the next upgrade two years later.

This trivial phone example can be applied to more epic illustrations as well, such as the Law of Sacrifice. John C. Maxwell coined this Law by explaining, "We need to give up to go up."[54] Giving up means letting go *first*, without the guarantee of anything in exchange. It's an act of faith that contains a real risk. Charles Du Bois referred to it as the ability "at any moment to sacrifice what we are for what we would become."[55]

Higher Life Design Travelers pack plenty of growth with them on their journey.

E = Enthusiastic

A few years ago at a leadership conference I attended, one of the exercises was to write out a statement that captured our *enthusiasm*. Unfamiliar with the etymology or exact definition of *enthusiasm*, I was shocked to discover the power behind those ten letters.

Enthusiasm is from the Greek word *enthousiasmos,* translated *en* "in" + *theos* "god." It means:

enthusiasm
1. divine inspiration
2. inspired or possessed by a god
3. to be in ecstasy

Talk about a powerful exercise! I went to work on a statement that reflected my divine inspiration and ecstasy. I came up with:

The supercharged experience of leading the cutting-edge.

Even today, when I read this statement my heart beats a little quicker and my adrenaline pumps a little faster. It defines who I am and what I love. I'll break down each word and tell you why it fires me up.

Supercharged

Step into my home office and you'll see dozens of model airplanes poised for takeoff. Maybe that's one of the reasons I love to travel. I'm addicted to the undeniable scream of the jet engine pushing away from the earth, lifting upward into unfamiliar skies.

Similarly, I enjoy the thrill of working with people poised for takeoff. I love the feeling of pushing away from self-limiting beliefs and mediocre living. I'm addicted to the Higher Life Design.

Experience

An old Chinese proverb says, "Tell me and I'll forget; show me and I may remember; involve me and I'll understand."[56]

In other words, a lecture doesn't influence as powerfully as an experience. Skydiving makes a great example. I can sit in a room and study the mechanics of skydiving. I can watch a video only of someone skydiving. Those lessons may help, but what cements skydiving in my head is actually jumping from a plane.

Similarly, my passion is to teach by involving others. Forget theory—I want to experience life firsthand—and so that's exactly what I do. I help my teams experience transformation, not merely talk about it.

Leading

From a young age, I've enjoyed the *privilege* and *responsibility* of leading others.

I say *privilege* because true leadership isn't something you get by position. Quite the opposite—it's something you earn with permission.

Similarly, I say *responsibility* because true leadership isn't exerting power. Quite the opposite—it's modeling servanthood.

Cutting-Edge

I'm a fan of technology and I respect innovation. Call me an early adopter, but I prefer cutting-edge rather than obsolete antique.

Even more than gadgets and gizmos, I prefer working with people who value cutting-edge. Innovation attracts a certain type of person. Some call them pioneers, entrepreneurs, or outliers. I call them friends.

Define Your Enthusiastic Statement

When you put together this whole statement, you can see a complete picture of my enthusiasm. I feel divinely inspired to devote my life to the

supercharged experience of leading the cutting-edge.

If you don't know your enthusiastic statement yet, I encourage you to take some time and develop one. Once you have it, write it out in the space below.

_____

_____

_____

_____

_____

_____

_____

_____

_____

_____

Higher Life Design Travelers pack plenty of enthusiasm with them on their journey.

You are What You Pack

No one will pack your suitcase for you. It's your choice what you bring: B.A.G.G.A.G.E. or L.U.G.G.A.G.E.

B. = Blame		L. = Loving
A. = Arrogance		U. = Unleashed
G. = Greed		G. = Gutsy
G. = Grudges	or	G. = Generous
A. = Apathy		A. = Active
G. = Grumbling		G. = Growing
E. = Envy		E. = Enthusiastic

One will weigh you down; the other will lift you up. One will inhibit your journey; the other will enhance it. Higher Life Design Travelers know the right packing eliminates the wrong baggage.

Higher Life Design Traveler's Checklist

☐   I don't BLAME people or circumstances so that I can take responsibility for my own life.

☐   I eradicate ARROGANCE from my life by serving others so I can create a lasting legacy.

☐   I eliminate GREED by giving to those in need.

☐   I release GRUDGES that hold me back so I can travel without being weighed down.

☐   I fight APATHY by getting more clarity surrounding my why.

☐   I overcome GRUMBLING by choosing to broadcast a positive frequency so I can attract quality relationships.

☐   I erase ENVY by adopting an abundant mindset so I will not poison my potential.

☐   I express and embody unconditional LOVE in my relationships.

☐   I live an UNLEASHED life that models authenticity so I inspire those around me to achieve more.

☐   I embrace a GUTSY attitude and run toward the battle so others will find courage when facing their own battle.

☐   I exemplify GENEROSITY by mentoring a few key people so I can return the generosity that has been given to me.

☐   I take an ACTIVE role in my personal health and wellness so I can have the stamina and energy to sustain the Higher Life.

☐ I invite change, knowing it is essential to keep GROWING so I keep expanding personally and professionally.

☐ I wrote a statement that captures my ENTHUSIASM so I clearly know what fuels me.

PART II

FLIGHT—*PREPARATION*

Step Three:
The Attitude Equation

Higher Altitude = Better Attitude

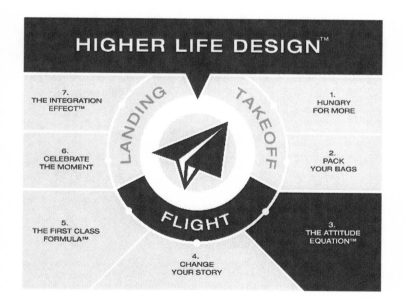

For the past five years, Jefferson's leadership and positive attitude have helped me Design a Higher Life. His story, his vision, and his first class attitude have been a beacon of inspiration for myself and thousands of others.

— George A.

Although I've always felt God placed something bigger inside of me, I gave up on my dreams. I became comfortable and accepted "the cards" I'd been dealt.

Jefferson Santos gave me hope by believing in me more than I believed in myself. Because of his mentorship, I've changed my future and my family's future.

Changing your mindset is critical to obtaining your dreams. I'm now convinced God has a Higher Life Design for everyone—including me.

— Shannon G.

"The toughest athlete in the world is a 62-year-old woman."[57]

This description, spoken in 2011, sounded accurate. Who else in their right mind would attempt to swim 110 miles from Cuba to Florida?

As could be expected, endurance swimmer Diana Nyad fell short of her goal. With this fourth failed attempt, most people would have quit forever. Not Nyad.

She first tried in 1978, nearly half a life earlier. At that time, she swam inside a 20×40 foot steel shark cage for nearly 42 hours. Strong westerly winds and eight-foot swells slammed against the cage. Although she made it 76 miles, her course proved anything but straight. She lost 29 pounds in less than two days of swimming before doctors made her stop.[58]

According to *New York Daily News*, "The elusive dream receded from the forefront of her mind but it never disappeared entirely. When Nyad turned 60, she started thinking about her limited time on this planet and could not forgive herself for the time she already wasted on negative thoughts."[59]

Nyad changed her *attitude* by changing her *altitude*. Through elevated thinking, she snapped out of her self-imposed rut. This renewed dream required unwavering passion and resolve. Her bigger vision demanded a better attitude. Negativity no longer hijacked her heart.

"The swim from Cuba to Florida, an old dream, came rushing back and electrified her imagination. She vowed, in her 60s, to conquer the seemingly insurmountable journey she failed to finish in her 20s."

In 2013, at the age of 64, Nyad achieved her dream, this time without using the protective cage.

Altitude Determines Attitude

You've probably heard the phrase, "Your attitude determines your altitude." In other words, the better your attitude is, the higher you'll go and the more you'll achieve. This statement contains some truth.

However, with my team I've flipped the phrase. I believe the higher your *altitude,* the better your *attitude.* I've seen firsthand that when Higher Life Design Travelers feel stuck, they change themselves by changing their focus. Elevated thinking demands a positive attitude.

Viktor Frankl (1905-1997) exemplified this principle during his time in a Nazi concentration camp. At Auschwitz, he was reduced to nothing but his "naked existence." Stripped of every comfort, the guards took his clothes, his wedding ring, and the manuscript of a book he was writing. "Then, every inch of his body was shaved as he was escorted into a shower room. His only consolation was that real water dripped from the shower heads instead of gas."[60]

Before prison, Frankl functioned as a psychotherapist and brain surgeon specializing in treating depression, especially for those prone to suicide. Conditions in Auschwitz were so extreme that many prisoners intentionally ended their lives. They wanted to escape the physical and mental torture so badly, they killed themselves. Eventually, abuse took its toll and sabotaged even the most positive attitude.

At times, even Frankl felt the allure of death—a place devoid of pain. To avoid this fate, Frankl kept himself alive by finding his own purpose—keeping other prisoners from committing suicide. He changed his *attitude* by changing his *altitude*.

Helping other prisoners find their purpose renewed his own sense of purpose. He motivated one prisoner by helping him dream of being reunited with his daughter. He inspired another to stay alive so he could complete his life's work one day. By helping prisoners identify their dreams, Frankl found his own dream.

The only *attitudes* that survived Auschwitz were the ones that soared above the prison walls. The *altitude* of the dream helped prisoners escape their horrific conditions.

Frankl famously wrote, "The one thing you can't take away from me is the way I choose to respond to what you do to me. The last of one's freedoms is to choose one's attitude in any given circumstance." [61]

He realized the potential of your attitude is directly shaped by the level of your altitude. Those who reached higher were the ones who went further and survived. Dreams matter, especially in a place like Auschwitz.

Become Like a Child

What about you? Do you struggle with a positive attitude? If so, quit focusing on your attitude and instead increase your altitude.

How big is your dream? Perhaps you've been aiming too low. Small dreams only require mediocre attitudes, but the biggest dreams evoke the best attitudes.

Maybe you don't know what your dream is. Inevitably when I talk about dreams, some people feel confused or embarrassed because they lack clarity. I'm motivated by people who don't know their dream, mainly because I believe dreams are planted in every person. I believe finding your dream is more about *recovery* then *discovery*.

Look at any child and you'll see three unique characteristics:

- Children love.
- Children take risks.
- Children dream.

LOVE: Children Give Affection

When my son, Harrison, was born, we didn't teach him how to cuddle. He did it quite naturally. I still remember him snuggling with his mommy. This affection isn't unique. Just watch young children at playtime. They hug each other before they part ways, even though they just met. Only as kids grow older, with strangers in mind, do they choose *not* to give affection freely.

RISK-TAKING: Children Take Action

Children know what they want and they go after it. If they're hungry for a cookie, they stand on a counter and jeopardize their safety for a few sugary calories. If they want to swim, they jump in a pool. They put action behind their ideas. Only as kids grow older, with the dangers of fire, water, and falling in mind, do they learn *not* to take risks.

DREAMING: Children See Higher

Children have a better idea of what they want than most adults. Kids see what *can* be and they're not afraid to tell you. When I ask young people about their dreams, they'll say, "I dream of playing football," or "I dream of being an artist" or "dancing" and so forth. Ask most adults, and they'll just cluelessly shrug their shoulders. Only as kids grow older and discover opposition do they learn *not* to dream.

Watch Out for the Monkeys

A quick look at a famous monkey experiment told by business professors Gary Hamel and C. K. Prahalad explains why most adults stop dreaming.

Researchers placed four monkeys in a room. In the center of the room was a tall pole with a bunch of bananas suspended from the top.

One of the hungry monkeys started climbing the pole to get something to eat, but just as he reached out to grab a banana, he was doused with a torrent of cold water. With a squeal, the monkey abandoned its quest and retreated down the pole. Each monkey made a similar attempt and each one was drenched with cold water. After making several attempts, they finally gave up on the irresistible bananas.

The researchers removed one of the monkeys from the room and replaced him with a new monkey. As the newcomer began to climb the pole, the other three grabbed him and pulled him down to the ground. After trying to climb the pole several times and being dragged down by the others, he finally gave up and never attempted to climb the pole again.

The researchers replaced the original monkeys, one by one, with new ones, and each time a new monkey was brought in, he would be dragged down by the others before he could reach the bananas. In time, only monkeys who had never received a cold shower were in the room, but none of them would climb the pole. They prevented one another from climbing, but none of them knew why. [62]

Because you were once a child, naturally you once dreamed. Somewhere along the way, you probably encountered pain. Maybe you failed. Maybe your dream was squashed. Maybe, like the monkey experiment, other people pushed you down and held you back.

It's time to recover your dream. Forget the excuses. Your *attitude* depends on your *altitude*. A small dream only produces a stunted attitude. However, "Xtreme Dreams" require incredible attitudes.

The Original Xtreme Dream

Most people think Diana Nyad's dream began when she was 28 years old and attempted to swim from Cuba to Florida the first time. A closer look reveals a different story. At that age—and with every other attempt—she experienced dream recovery, not dream discovery.

"Nyad remembers dreaming about swimming across the Florida Straits during her first visit to Cuba before the Communist takeover when she was 8 years old."[63]

Often, dreams fade over time, hiding in your subconscious only to come raging back into your awareness later in life.

Nyad knew this better than most. She said, "You have a dream...that doesn't come to fruition, but you move on with life. But it's somewhere back there. Then you turn 60, and your mom just dies, and you're looking for something. And the dream comes waking out of your imagination."[64]

If you search on Google for the term, "Xtreme Dream" the top search result will likely produce Diana Nyad's website.[65] When you visit her site, you'll see a map with Cuba at the bottom and Key West, Florida at the top. A red line connects the two land masses. Along the way, you'll notice orange dots with brief commentaries from her "Xtreme Dream Team" about Diana's progress. At one of the final orange dots—dated 3:06 p.m. Eastern Time on September 3, 2013—her team posted:

"Diana arrives in Key West after swimming 52 Hours 54 Minutes 18.6 Seconds and 110.4 statute miles."

Watching the video of her final steps walking onto shore felt symbolic. During those few minutes, I felt I was watching a story about humanity, not just about sports. Nyad appeared disoriented at first. I guess 52 hours of swimming has that effect. A crowd of people surrounded her. They showed up to cheer for her in the midst of her "Xtreme Dream."

According to the rules, no one can assist her on her journey out of the water. With her balance extremely challenged, Nyad stood with intense effort. She fell several times. Though each step looked painful, the emotion of the moment can't be captured in words. The altitude of her "Xtreme Dream" inspired a superhuman attitude.

With her last step, the crowd erupted and celebrated the victory right along with her. Though some naysayers criticized the hype, Nyad achieved a dream that infected her since the age of eight. With microphones hanging on her every word, Nyad managed to communicate a few powerful phrases in spite of all her pain:

"I got three messages: One is—we should never, ever give up.
Two is—you never are too old to chase your dreams.
Three is—it looks like a solitary sport, but it's a team."[66]

When asked what motivated her to keep going she said,

"This is a lifelong dream of mine…. We blink and another decade passes. I don't want to reach the end of my life and regret not having given my days everything in me to make them worthwhile."

Three Truths about Xtreme Dreams

Higher Life Design Travelers think higher and dream bigger. Their lofty altitude evokes a better attitude.

If you suffer from a negative attitude, change your altitude. Recover an old dream you lost somewhere along the way. Then apply these three truths from Nyad's celebration speech.

1. Never, Ever Give Up: Find a Way to Win

In life, you'll find whatever you seek. If you want to quit, you'll discover reasons to quit. If you want to win, you'll find a way. It's your choice.

I love the statement, "Set a goal so big that you can't achieve it until you grow into the person who can." This means that an Xtreme Dream isn't an end. Instead, it's merely a pathway for you to reach your potential. It forces you to dig deep and experience transformation. If you could do it easily, it wouldn't be a dream, only a task.

On *CBS This Morning*, Nyad said her mantra through the swim was, "Find a way." Referring to the journey, she said, "It doesn't matter…what you come up against because none of it's going to be pleasant. You're hardly ever out there going, 'Isn't it a beautiful moon tonight?' The crew is feeling that, but you're kind of suffering through the whole thing…and this is why people are relating to my story—all of us suffer heartache. All of us suffer difficulties in our lives, and if you say to yourself, 'Find a way,' you'll make it through."[67]

2. You're Never Too Old to Chase Your Dreams: Eliminate Every Excuse

One of my mentors, John C. Maxwell, told me, "Excuses are merely exit ramps on the highway to your dreams." Trust me; there are millions of these ramps. Sometimes I think people who achieve their dreams are simply the ones who didn't quit.

Limitations are merely lies we believe about ourselves. I know of Ernestine Shepherd, a 75-year-old bodybuilding grandmother.[68] I know of Nick Vujicic, a man without any limbs who swims, paints, plays soccer, and speaks to millions of people.[69]

What's your excuse?

Nyad had every reason to quit. She could have taken the "I'm too old" exit ramp or even the "Jellyfish stung my face" exit ramp, but she didn't. Despite failing four times, she dropped her excuses and continued down the highway of her dream. And on September 3, 2013, she reached her final destination.

3. It Looks Like a Solitary Sport, but It's a Team: Build Your "Xtreme Dream Team"

Swimming from Cuba to Florida felt so big, Nyad coined it her "Xtreme Dream." She needed a team to achieve this epic dream and she chose more than 40 people to help. Sensing the altitude of her dream inspired an incredible attitude within her team. They answered the call with strong belief and fierce determination, and because they all paid the price, they all experienced the payoff.

Every "Xtreme Dream" needs an "Xtreme Dream Team." I have big dreams. My team is currently more than 100,000 people strong and growing daily. The cool thing is that we're all working toward the same goal. Although this "Xtreme Dream" requires energy and effort, it also provides us high returns and generous rewards.

It's Called the "Higher Life Design" for a Reason

By investing time in reading this book and growing yourself, I can already tell something about your altitude. You think higher than most.

I also know you're passionate about being more, doing more, having more, and giving more. Regardless, I want to challenge you to think even higher. It takes no more energy to think bigger. And higher thinking is essential for achieving more because higher altitudes evoke better attitudes.

Take a deep breath. You've come a long way already.

In our journey thus far, you raised your expectations in the Takeoff Phase. You got Hungry for More (Step One) and Packed Your Bags (Step Two). In this Flight Phase, you've prepared by using The Attitude Equation (Step Three).

In a moment we'll take the next step—Change Your Story (Step Four). Each of these seven steps that compose the Higher Life Design are essential. You're not allowed to skip some or avoid others. Doing so will only hinder your height.

All seven steps in the Higher Life Design will help you arrive at your intended destination healthy, wealthy, and happy. Before you take any other step, be sure to complete the following checklist.

Higher Life Design Traveler's Checklist

☐ I change my attitude by changing my altitude so I can go higher.

☐ I take complete responsibility for my attitude so I won't self-sabotage my results.

☐ I invest more time in dream recovery than in dream discovery so I can get in touch with my internal drives and motivations.

☐ I love more by giving affection to those closest to me so they will feel valued.

☐ I take more risk by acting upon my desires so I won't have a life of regret.

☐ I dream more by elevating my thinking so I can achieve more.

☐ I find a way to win so I can overcome obstacles.

☐ I eliminate every excuse so I don't become a quitter.

☐ I've identified my Xtreme Dream so I can start living life bigger and bolder.

☐ I built an Xtreme Dream Team so I can make my Xtreme Dream possible.

☐ I will continue with the Higher Life Design and complete all seven steps so I will arrive at my intended destination healthy, wealthy, and happy.

STEP FOUR:
CHANGE YOUR STORY

To change yourself, you must
first change your story

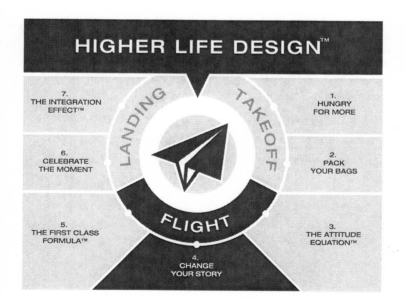

Five years ago, I had stale dreams. I felt as though the next big chapter in my life was moving up to management and running a bunch of other employees. Before I met Jefferson, I was on the same treadmill as everyone I knew, running a race that led me nowhere.

Three years after taking on a different mindset, I received three big promotions at work. I began to believe in myself and see myself as a champion. I now look at the "mountains" in front of me as a way to grow stronger.

I recently decided I was better at creating my family's future and I left the corporate world. Now I get to be a dad, a real husband, and the man God made me to be.
— **Jared G.**

I've always had big dreams and set big goals of what I wanted to accomplish in life. My problem was that I never had the right tracks to run on to accomplish those goals and dreams.

Jefferson showed me a system that has allowed me to accomplish my life purpose. Best of all, I feel truly fulfilled knowing I now have the freedom of choice.
— **Ivan L.**

"I don't like the cards I've been dealt," the man said to me with a tone of defeat.

I let his words pass through my ears and into my awareness.

I felt sorry for him—but not for reasons you might expect. Although he had obvious challenges, like all of us do, I pitied him for another reason. I saw myself in his statement. I used to think like him, *before* I changed my story.

When I lived with my mom in her apartment I told myself something similar—I didn't like the cards I'd been dealt, either.

Then one day things changed.

I paid off all my debts and moved to my own place.

I traveled the world.

I built an international team.

I met Megan, my brilliant and beautiful wife.

I became one of the top leaders in the company.

From an outside perspective, it looked like everything just happened all at once, kind of by accident. Some said my luck changed. Others said life dealt me a new hand. These comments sounded plausible, but they were simply inaccurate.

The first change happened inside me long before my circumstances changed. I changed my story first and, as a result, I changed myself.

Rather than feeling bitter about the cards dealt to me, I realized I could get a new hand. Even better, I discovered I could actually *become the dealer* in my life.

This new story gave me a new awareness. Until then, I wanted new results but—truth be told—I didn't think I was worthy of those results. With some deeper digging, I learned I'd never outperform my own self-image.

If I saw myself as a 60 on a 100-point scale, the world wasn't going to raise my value. I came to learn that thermostats and self-image have a bunch in common. If you're set at 60 internally, you'll never reach 100 externally. Even if people around you compliment you or give you a raise, your results will always drop back to 60—the exact setting of your self-image.

Early in my career, I wanted great results, but a closer look proved I wasn't designed for them. My self-image was set too low. I might have hoped and wished, but hope isn't a strategy and wishing doesn't change reality. I needed to reprogram my results by first rewriting my story.

This new story helped me change the way I saw myself. In a matter of a few short months, my results began to reflect this new self-image. I had a different experience because I told myself a different story.

A Lesson from a Young Lion Cub

These days, I find myself consuming an entirely different kind of entertainment—cartoons and children's stories. Remember, I'm the father of two young sons. This entertainment is fun and light, but if you look deep enough and listen close enough, you'll find the Higher Life Design. I often see it in the movies I watch and in the stories I hear.

One example involves a young lion cub. Although you might know the movie, you've probably never seen the principle. You can see step four—Change Your Story—in the life of Simba, the main character in Disney's *The Lion King*. This lion changed himself only after he changed his story.

In the story, we meet Mufasa—king of the jungle, ruler over all. At the beginning of the story, he and his son, Simba, had a beautiful relationship. The world felt perfect. Simba loved wrestling with his mighty father and dreaming about his place in the circle of life.

Like every prince, Simba knew he was destined for a Higher Life—a life where he'd one day rule the jungle as king. His parents told him this story ever since the day he drew breath. They daily reinforced this story, just in case he ever had doubts.

Because he had a healthy relationship with his father, Simba also had a healthy self-image. He felt royal blood pumping through his veins. Though young and scrawny, with each passing day, he became older and stronger.

Then it happened. His story changed drastically, largely by his own doing. One day Simba listened to his deceiving uncle, Scar, and placed himself in great danger—right in the middle of a wildebeest stampede in a deep ravine with no way out for the little cub. After being alerted that Simba was in danger, Mufasa raced to his rescue, stepped in harm's way, then sacrificed his own life to save his son.

Following his father's death, Simba's ideal story changed. This wasn't supposed to happen. He immediately felt guilt and shame for the foolish choice that cost his father's life. Simba believed it was entirely his fault, ignorant of the fact that Scar set the stampede in motion and killed Mufasa to steal his brother's throne.

Listening again to Scar's advice, Simba ran away—from himself and from his bigger story. Rather than embrace the names "Son" and "King," Simba adopted other names like "Murderer" and "Failure." Rather than embrace the bigger story that he was the lion king, the rightful leader, he adopted a different one called "hakuna matata." This Swahili phrase can be translated literally as "no worries." It means "don't worry, be happy."[70]

Simba learned this new "hakuna matata" story from Timon and Pumbaa, his new friends in the jungle. With low expectations, they simply cruised through life without a care in the world. Simba enjoyed this smaller story because it helped him erase the shame and guilt.

Over time, though, no matter how he tried to embrace this story of purposelessness, he couldn't shake the epic one that kept calling to him. It infected him and weighed heavy on his heart. Finally, after running for years, he reached the end of himself.

His breakthrough came crashing into him, literally, via a crazy baboon named Rafiki. This messenger confronted Simba in the midst of his identity crisis and led him through the jungle to a pond where he saw his father's image in his own reflection.

Overwhelmed, Simba ran to an open field where, in an honest and humble moment, he vulnerably cried out to the heavens:

"You said you'd always be there for me, but you're not.
It's because of me. It's my fault."

Amazingly, a ghostly image of his father appeared above him. Simba poured out his heart to his father. He told him the small story he had adopted. He confessed his inadequacies, his shortcomings, and his hang-ups. His father listened to his story, but then spoke boldly:

> *"You are more than what you have become.*
> *…Remember who you are."*[71]

Mufasa reminded Simba of the true story inside him—not the cheap substitute he told himself and everyone else. When Simba changed his story, only then could he change himself, embrace his true identity, and accept the crown that was rightfully his.

By reclaiming the bigger story he found new courage to confront Scar and redeem his destiny in the process. He became the rightful heir and the lion king—taking his place in the circle of life.

Defy Your Small Story with a Bigger S.T.O.R.Y.

Within this example we witness a powerful principle. In the beginning, Simba seemed self-assured and confident. He understood his destiny. Yet in a very short time, his story changed, and so did he.

With this new self-image set extremely low, his results followed suit. This child of the king forgot who he was and what he was about. Rather than embracing royalty, he found himself surrounded by friends who found pleasure in underperforming. Instead of being different, he found acceptance in embracing their story of careless living and a worry-free existence.

Eventually, Simba experienced transformation. His *defining* moment became his *defying* moment. The change took place when he rejected his small story and embraced his bigger one instead. His strategy was simple. To change himself, he first changed his S.T.O.R.Y.

I've developed a framework around the example of Simba. I've used it within my own life and when coaching others. If you apply this five-step framework, you'll be able to change yourself too. It's the predictable conclusion of the bigger S.T.O.R.Y.

Change Yourself: Change Your S.T.O.R.Y.

S = **S**hare Your Emotion

T = **T**ravel Deep Inside

O = **O**vercome the Accusers

R = **R**emember the Truth

Y = **Y**ield for No One

Let's explore each step.

S = Share Your Emotion

Oftentimes, stories sabotage success because we keep them hidden. Simba let his guilt and shame grow by refusing to share it with others. Denial doesn't erase the pain or the power your story holds over you.

The first step toward changing your story is to share your emotion. ""Hakuna matata"—"don't worry, be happy"— did nothing for Simba. It kept him captive by providing a convenient mask behind which he could hide.

As a society, we often downplay emotions and disregard feelings. Boys are told not to cry and adults curb emotion through casually written prescriptions that merely numb feelings.

Emotion is one of the key qualities that make us human. Stifling it only strengthens the power of your small story. By sharing emotion, you'll rediscover your voice and reclaim the bigger story inside you.

T = Travel Deep Inside

Most people don't like to look inside. Simba certainly didn't. They think by ignoring the bigger story, the pain of regret won't feel as strong. This isn't true.

Simba knew he couldn't ignore his bigger story forever, and running away didn't allow him to escape the problem or the pain. Rafiki took him through the dark, dense jungle and straight into his pain. As he traveled inside he felt worse— initially. Although only a brief journey, it still wasn't easy. Branches smacked his face and vines tripped his legs.

This uncharted territory feels scary at first, but traveling inside makes us release control—a prerequisite for transformation. Growth only occurs when we're stretched beyond what's comfortable and familiar. Although Simba didn't enjoy the pain of being stretched, it felt better than the pain of a small story.

O = *Overcome the Accusers*

Just like us, Simba heard accusations—both externally and internally. Scar may have started the verbal venom, but Simba finished the fight. Simba may have fled from Scar, but he couldn't escape the voices inside his head.

Because Rafiki knew this, he led Simba to the end of himself. Using a pond as a mirror, he made Simba look at himself. Rather than seeing confidence or acceptance, Simba only observed disgust and disappointment.

Knowing the significance of a healthy self-image, Rafiki made Simba look again. By looking deeper, Simba saw someone greater.

You'll only overcome these adversaries by letting them express their accusations. Your strength comes as a result of standing firm in spite of their attacks. By stepping toward the battle, you'll inevitably win the war.

R = *Remember the Truth*

My favorite teacher said, "The truth will set you free."[72] He spoke this more than 2,000 years ago to a group of people enslaved by lies. Their prejudices prevented them from seeing truth and experiencing freedom.

Lies often do this. They blind you from your possibilities and potential. They keep you playing safe and playing small. They make you forget about the bigger story that calls your name.

Simba experienced this firsthand. He needed a truth teller to shake him up and wake him up. Mufasa put it straight to his son by saying:

*"You have forgotten who you are
and so have forgotten me."*[73]

He reminded him of the truth:

*"You are my son and the one true king.
Remember who you are."*[74]

This truth unlocked Simba from his fear and unleashed him into his future. He left that truth encounter with a renewed sense of passion and purpose.

You need your own truth encounter. You need a truth teller to shake you up and wake you up. You need someone to tell you:

*"You are more than what you have become.
…Remember who you are."*[75]

This is your moment. There's a whole group of people waiting for you to get past what you're waiting for. It's time for you to renew your sense of passion and purpose.

Y = Yield for Nobody

Reclaiming his bigger story meant confronting Scar—the one who tried to steal it from him. Although Simba might have felt a little fearful, he didn't let it show. His most difficult work had already been done. The hardest work is always what we do on the inside—not the outside. Simba had:

- S hared his emotion.
- T raveled deep inside.
- O vercome his accusers.
- R emembered the truth.

He was a different lion now. He changed himself by changing his S.T.O.R.Y. The only thing left to do was reclaim his throne. To do so, he had to

- Y ield for no one—including Scar.

Unfortunately, Scar wasn't about to step aside without a fight. He tried different tactics to shut Simba up and put him down. Initially, he went for what worked in the past—shame and blame. In front of his friends and loved ones, Scar made Simba admit he killed his father.

To Scar's surprise, Simba stood his ground. He confessed his previous mistake, ready to admit what he thought was the truth without worrying how the others responded. In the past, he might have fled, but in this bigger story Scar didn't have a chance.

As a result, Scar first resorted to violence. Then he fought and pleaded. He eventually cheated—throwing hot coals at Simba's face. In the midst of their brawl, truth broke through the surface. Scar admitted he was the murderer. He had killed Mufasa to secure the throne for himself.

Courage filled Simba the moment truth emerged. Scar's reign was over. With one final display of strength, Simba threw

Scar off a cliff along with the small story that had haunted him for years.

A Higher Life Requires a Bigger Story

You are more than the story you've told yourself. As long as you're still breathing, you have the opportunity to embrace your bigger story. It all begins by following the five-step framework. Here are a few quick action steps and questions to get you started:

Share Your Emotion

Get a journal. Write freely. Don't judge. Capture your thoughts. Forget critique. Ask questions. Shout to the Heavens. Express yourself. Identify areas of emotion. Trace their origin.

Is there anger? If so, what's your blocked goal?

Is there sadness? If so, what's the loss you experienced?

Is there regret? If so, what's the opportunity you missed?

Travel Deep Inside

Get ready for an adventure. Prepare yourself for the journey within. Branches may smack you. Vines may trip you. Uncharted territory might feel scary at first, but take courage— you're growing.

What has avoiding your bigger story cost you?

What moves you and motivates you?

From what are you running?

Overcome the Accusers

Do you have enemies? Good! You stood up for something in your life.

Do you have accusers? Great! People don't attack someone who's not a threat.

Haters may have started the verbal venom, but you need to finish the fight. You must escape the voices inside your head. Step towards the battle to inevitably win the war. Replace their lies with your true destiny.

It's time to reach the end of yourself.

It's time to embrace a healthy self-image.

It's time to look deeper and see something greater

Remember the Truth

Lies blind you. Truth frees you. Don't allow your prejudices to prevent you from seeing truth and experiencing freedom. Don't be blinded from your possibilities and potential.

Don't forget who you are.

Remember your bigger story.

Become who you were born to be.

Yield for No One

Prepare to stand your ground. Prepare to be shamed and blamed. Prepare to confess previous mistakes. In the past you might have fled, but in this bigger story apathy doesn't have a chance.

Yield for nobody. They may fight.

Yield for nobody. They many plead.

Yield for nobody. They may cheat.

Pregnant in the Rain in Venice

Step four—Change Your Story—obviously pertains to epic situations like destiny and legacy, but it also pertains to everyday situations like getting lost in Venice.

Megan, my wife, was five months pregnant and we couldn't find our hotel. Making matters worse, it began to rain. Our roller bags didn't make our journey any easier. We walked up and down the sidewalk wet, lost, and frustrated.

I found myself telling and retelling a negative story. I let circumstances get the best of me. My crummy attitude soon reflected the crummy weather. Our Venice story was almost hijacked by bad weather and bad attitudes.

Thankfully, I caught myself. I knew if I wanted to change myself I needed to change my story.

Just then, I looked up and saw a beautiful bakery. Megan led the way and we stepped inside to get dry. The kind owner gave us directions to our hotel. In a matter of minutes, we located our mini oasis and stepped out of the rain for good.

With stomachs rumbling, we looked at the clock. Southern European dining doesn't kick off until 8:00 p.m. and it was much earlier so we had no other choice. Famished from our journey through the rain, we raided the mini bar in our hotel room. Hardly Italian food at its finest, we dined on Pringles® and peanuts. Our frustration turned into laughter as we playfully fought over the snack food we just scored.

To this day, we still chuckle at the memory of our random Italian feast. Without much effort, we could have clung to a small story that cold, rainy evening. Instead, we replaced it with a bigger one.

That trip to Venice now ranks as one of my favorites. We even returned to the beautiful bakery before we flew home. We both enjoyed the most amazing macaroons—completely in a class all their own. Looking back, we would never have found those macaroons if the rain didn't force us into the bakery that evening. Sometimes the tastiest stories start out in ways you never would have chosen.

Higher Life Design Traveler's Checklist

☐ I am the dealer of my own destiny so I don't get stuck.

☐ I reset my self-image so I can help serve more people.

☐ I changed myself by first changing my story.

☐ I don't run away from my bigger story because I've embraced my true calling.

☐ I don't hang out with underperformers because I don't want to be one myself.

☐ I've defied my small story so I can invite my defining moment.

☐ I've rediscovered my voice by choosing to share my emotions.

☐ I've traveled deep inside because running away doesn't solve the problem or the pain.

☐ I've overcome my accusers so I don't live as someone who's intimidated.

☐ I remember the truth so I am not blinded by the lies.

☐ I don't yield to my "haters" so I can live authentically instead.

☐ I've changed my story in both epic and everyday situations because every detail matters.

Step Five:
The First Class Formula

Never second guess the power of first class

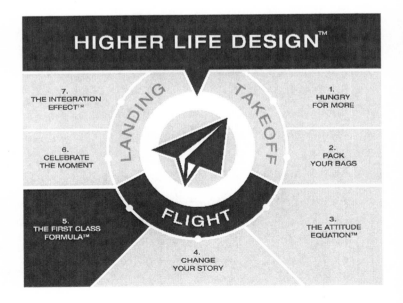

I can't tell you how freeing it feels to live every day without worrying about money. It's like a big iron rod has been lifted off my shoulders.

I'm so glad Jefferson didn't give up on his dreams. He's taught me that to win at a very high level, I have to be willing to go through an incredible journey!

— **Srinivas B.**

Four years ago, Jefferson Santos mentored my wife regarding our new business venture. He encouraged us to attend an upcoming personal development seminar. In my mind I ruled it out because of the cost measured in dollars and hours.

I had a broke mindset at the time and Jefferson asked me, "Do you want the lifestyle I have?" Then he challenged me, "If the answer is 'Yes,' you need to do what I have done and attend."

Thank the Lord he was willing to stretch our limiting beliefs. We did attend that life-changing weekend. I look back on that seminar as a turning point in our lives and in our business. Just three short months later, my wife was able to leave her corporate job and now we are both pursing a lifestyle that we are passionate about.

Although life always has its struggles, Jefferson taught us by example to always keep a first class mindset and realize that anything is possible. We can't thank him enough for the impact he has had in our life. He's a great role model, a true friend, and a wise mentor.

— **Daniel R.**

I 've always loved airplanes, even from a young age. Some friends say I was destined to love them because of Jefferson Airplane, the 1960s psychedelic rock band. Although we share a common first name, my love for flying even eclipsed an award-winning rock band.

Buckle up: here's that story.

First Time Airborne

I vividly remember my first plane ride. Everything appealed to me, including the preflight instructions about oxygen masks and flotation devices. I happily and hungrily consumed the drinks and snacks delivered by the flight attendant. I'm a little embarrassed to say I even found the whole toilet concept a bit fascinating. (Where did all that "stuff" go when I flushed?)

For a kid, these questions and details only add to the mystique of flying. It's unbelievable enough that you can strap yourself into a seat and fly through the air at 500 miles per hour. I'm still perplexed that in a matter of hours, you can arrive at a destination which used to take several days to reach by car.

Yes, from the very first minute I stepped onto an airplane, I was hooked.

Today, if you visited my office you'd see bookshelves accented with 109 model airplanes. Fighter planes, jet planes, and prop planes—I have them all. I guess I like a visual reminder that life *above* the clouds feels incredibly inspiring, especially when sitting in first class.

The Four Stages of Competence

It probably sounds funny, but in my first few years as an air traveler, I didn't even know first class existed. Still a newbie, I needed to learn a few things about the friendly skies. Initially, I simply boarded the plane in ignorance of this other world. Rather unaware, I assumed the people in the front of the plane just got there earlier than the rest of us. At this stage, I was what psychologists call *unconscious incompetent*. I didn't know any differently because I didn't know what I didn't know.

Eventually, I learned all about first class. I'll "blame" it on the passenger who sat next to me on one particular flight. She told me all about the wonderful benefits. According to her, first class passengers enjoyed luxury, space, comfort, service, and privacy. With a little more research I learned the experience in first class varies with each airline and aircraft.

On a Boeing 747, for example, first class provides large reclining seats, a workstation, and TV in a space surrounded by privacy dividers. On some longer flights, you might enjoy facilities similar to a five-star hotel, such as a mini-bar.

Recently, some airlines have transformed their first class sections into suites. On Singapore Airlines, passengers can sleep on a comfortable bed with a plush mattress. Suites located in the center can form a double bed after the privacy blinds between them are retracted into the ceiling—not a bad setup.

Something changed in me once I learned about first class. I was what psychologists call *conscious incompetent*. At this stage, I knew more. I was aware of what I lacked and boy did my awareness hurt.

Once I knew about first class, of course I wanted to fly in it. Until this point, I only experienced second class or "coach" as the airlines eloquently call it.

When I lived in my mother's apartment (haunted by her unforgiving mailbox), first class felt like an impossible dream. I'd board the plane and walk by it slowly. I wondered, what would it feel like to sit there?

Sure, they had more legroom, privacy, and comfort, but they also seemed to have something else. Call it a first class mindset. Although I couldn't explain it at the time, I knew I didn't have it yet.

A huge fan of flying, I wanted to experience the blue skies in style. First class seemed like the fastest way to fulfill that desire, and the Higher Life Design made that desire my reality.

I remember booking my inaugural first class flight. I felt the same excitement I did when I flew for the first time as a kid. I savored every moment, especially when reclining in my comfortable seat. More than just a different position on the plane, this specific flight represented a higher level for me personally.

At this stage, I was what psychologists call *conscious competent*. I was now aware of my new experience.

Fast-forward life through dozens upon dozens of flights and you might say I've changed. Rather than an occasional first class flight, now it's all I know. (I don't share this to brag, but to remind myself that achieving goals is possible.)

At this stage, I am what psychologists call *unconscious competent*. I no longer focus on first class. It's now part of who

I am. This new stage doesn't mean everything is easy. It simply means I no longer need to make first class a conscious effort.

When a certain athlete or musician reaches a level of mastery, observers sometimes make an interesting comment. They say, "It's so easy for her; she's just a natural."

Although this comment is kind, it's also ignorant. True, these observers recognize and appreciate the unconscious competence they see. But remember, masters don't start here. Rather, they arrive here by moving through what psychologists call the four stages of competence or the conscious competence learning model.

The Four Stages of Competence

1. Unconscious Incompetence
2. Conscious Incompetence
3. Conscious Competence
4. Unconscious Competence

Be encouraged—everyone has multiple areas of unconscious competence. But also realize that unconscious incompetence visits us all too. The good news is you can apply this model to most everything in life. One example is driving a car.

Driver's Education is a Good Thing

My son, Harrison, can't drive a car yet. That's a good thing. He's not even two years old. Presently, when Megan and I drive him around, he simply sits in his car seat. Although he enjoys the ride, he has no idea that one day he'll ever operate a vehicle. Referencing our model, he's *unconscious incompetent.*

I'm told—by people who have been parents much longer than I have been—that before I know it, Harrison will enter his teen years. When he does, he'll become aware he can't legally drive a car yet. Regardless if he'd like to debate the point, at this stage he'll be *consciously incompetent.*

A few years later, he'll reach the age when he's ready to take a driver's education class. He'll study rules of the road, accumulate observation hours, and master the NEW recommended hand positions on the steering wheel: "9 and 3."[76] If the Department of Motor Vehicles determines him worthy of a driver's license, Harrison will reach the stage of *conscious competent.*

Given enough time behind the wheel, Harrison will evolve to the stage of most drivers: *unconscious competent.* He'll drive across town without even consciously thinking about it. Utilizing his reflexes, he'll move his eyes from rearview mirror to driver's side mirror. He'll engage in a conversation on his cell phone by using a hands free device.

Harrison will have traveled through the four stages of competence. As a result, he'll also travel safely on the road and reach his intended destination.

The path through the four stages of competence looks something like this:

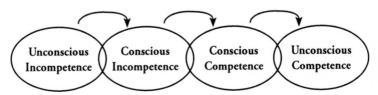

Are You an Outlier?

Unconscious competence sounds easy, and in many ways it should be—at least for those who put in the required time.

Malcom Gladwell, author of *Outliers,* refers to the "10,000-Hour Rule" throughout his book. The rule is based on a study by Dr. Anders Ericsson.[77] Gladwell explains the key to exceptional success in any field—the key to becoming an outlier—is, to a large extent, a matter of practicing a specific task for a total of around 10,000 hours. He references many examples from music, technology, and writing to support the premise.

Let's look at one example from each area.

Music

Example: The Beatles

The Beatles performed live in Hamburg, Germany more than 1,200 times from 1960 to 1964, thereby meeting the 10,000-Hour Rule. (They clocked thousands of hours just practicing for those 1,200 shows.) Gladwell asserts all the time The Beatles spent performing shaped their talent. He quotes The Beatles' biographer Philip Norman, "So by the time they returned to England from Hamburg, Germany, they sounded like no one else. It was the making of them."[78]

Technology

Example: Bill Gates

Gates met the 10,000-Hour Rule when he gained access to a high school computer in 1968 at the age of 13 and spent 10,000 hours programming on it. In *Outliers,* Gladwell interviewed Gates, who said that unique access to a computer at a time when they were not commonplace helped him succeed. Without that access, Gladwell states Gates would still be "a highly intelligent, driven, charming person and a successful professional," but he might not be worth $50 billion.

Writing

Example: Malcom Gladwell

The author himself states it took him exactly 10 years to meet the 10,000-Hour Rule, including his brief tenure at *The American Spectator* and his more recent work at *The Washington Post.* Although Gladwell doesn't mention it in his own book, he's become an outlier in his own industry. In 2005, he was named by *Time* magazine as one of the 100 Most Influential People. His books *The Tipping Point, Blink,* and *Outliers* each achieved *New York Times* bestseller status.

Become an Outlier in First Class Living

Becoming an outlier in driving cars, playing music, creating computers, and writing books is one thing, but becoming an outlier in first class living is an entirely different thing. One brings you *only* success. The other brings you success *and* significance. Higher Life Design Travelers achieve both.

The First Class Formula

To become an outlier in first class living and experience both success *and* significance, you must implement the First Class Formula. By using it, you'll be able to answer:

- **The WHAT**—By defining WHAT First Class living is
- **The WHY**—By discerning WHY you should join First Class living
- **The HOW**—By discovering HOW to join First Class living

To achieve first class living, let's unpack this formula in more depth.

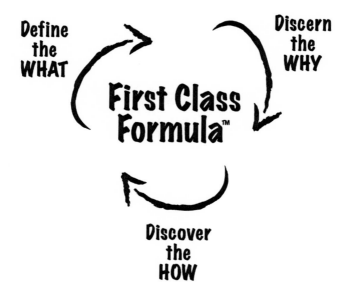

Define the WHAT: What First Class Living Is

In my company, we often talk about the goal of becoming a "master in the art of living." My friend and mentor Wayne Nugent introduced me to this concept. He's written the book on the topic—literally. The first time I heard it, I perked up.

Back then, the only first class living I knew was my position on an airplane. Intuitively, I knew this term meant much more than where I sat.

After some deeper exploration, I discovered the term "master in the art of living" originated from an author named L. P. Jacks. He defined this term as follows:

> *"A master in the art of living draws no sharp distinction between his work and his play; his labor and his leisure; his mind and his body; his education and his recreation. He hardly knows which is which. He simply pursues his vision of excellence through whatever he is doing, and leaves others to determine whether he is working or playing. To himself, he always appears to be doing both."*[79]

Notice the nuances within the words he used. Personally, by meditating upon each phrase, I've discovered lessons of both inspiration and education. Some of these thoughts are below. Feel free to record your own, too. Those are the thoughts that matter most.

"...no sharp distinction"—Imagine an integrated life, without walls or masks.

"...between his work and his play" —There are no "have to's here.

"...[between] his mind and his body" —Health is holistic, not compartmentalized.

"...[between] his education and his recreation"—Forget vacation days; learning is a life-long pursuit.

"…hardly knows which is which"—No need for categories. No need for confusion.

"…pursues his vision of excellence"—Eliminate labor; experience love.

"…through whatever he is doing"—Life is engaging because you are engaged.

"…leaves others to determine"—Self-evaluation matters; people pleasing doesn't.

"…whether he is working or playing"—People can't figure out someone who is truly integrated.

"…To himself"—You are the CEO of a cool little company called YOU.

"…he always appears to be doing both"—Masters in the art of living are fully present.

Write your thoughts below about being a "master in the art of living."

_____

_____

_____

_____

_____

_____

_____

_____

_____

_____

_____

_____

_____
_____
_____
_____
_____
_____
_____
_____
_____
_____
_____
_____
_____
_____
_____
_____
_____
_____
_____
_____
_____
_____
_____
_____
_____
_____
_____
_____
_____
_____

Discern the WHY:
Why You Should Join First Class Living

Joining first class living has its advantages.

Sitting in first class *on an airplane* offers you luxury, space, service, and privacy. Obviously, these perks enhance your *travel* experience.

Sitting in first class *in life* offers you even better rewards. These enhance your entire *life* experience. I call these perks The First Class Five.

The First Class Five

---

1. Connections

2. Counsel

3. Clarity

4. Competence

5. Confidence

Understanding each of these perks will help you discern WHY you should join first class living. Be warned, though—if you've been conditioned to overvalue fairness, some of these perks may rub you the wrong way.

I know when I initially heard about these first class perks, I didn't think they were "fair" either. However, taking a deeper dive into the topic of fairness revealed that much of life isn't "fair." Because of this possibility, I encourage you to suspend your "fair" meter for the present moment.

Society taught you to value fairness—and that's a good thing. However, fairness has its proper context.

It isn't fair only some people get into Harvard.

It isn't fair not everyone can play in the NFL.

It isn't fair some people can't afford to eat at elite restaurants.

It isn't fair only one person wins a spelling bee.

It isn't fair not everyone passes medical school.

It isn't fair you can't drive as fast as you want.

I could elaborate, but I think you get the point. Although I believe in "fairness," I also believe "fairness" must be viewed in its proper context. If not, society crumbles.

With that view of fairness in mind, let's explore The First Class Five.

Connections

I'll say it bluntly. If you want to be a loser, stay connected with losers. However, if you want to be a winner, stay connected with winners.

Just look around. People usually connect with like-minded people. Studies have shown that you become like the people with whom you associate. Why wouldn't you? By examining the pattern below, it all makes sense:

- Connections influence friendships.
- Friendships influence conversations.
- Conversations influence thoughts.
- Thoughts influence actions.
- Actions influence behavior.
- Behaviors influence results.

The bottom line is if you want different results, you need different connections. By joining first class, you'll naturally connect with other first class people.

Darren Hardy, publisher of *Success* magazine, called these first class connections "a high-achieving reference group."[80] Hardy explained, "As human beings, we raise or lower our performance to match the expectations and performance level of our reference group."

In other words, first class outliers seek out other first class outliers. This doesn't mean some people have more value than others. Although all people are created equal, everybody gets different results. The beggar and the President of the United States are both entrusted with the same amount of hours every week. Despite this, their results drastically differ.

First class connections will push you closer to first class results.

Counsel

Ancient wisdom says, "In the multitude of counsel is much wisdom."[81] Clearly, someone with counsel benefits greatly. However, not all counsel is equal. First class outliers have access to first class counsel. Although it may seem "unfair", these outliers can employ the best doctors, advisors, coaches, gurus, experts, and educators.

Although most everyone wants to get better, outliers have an extra advantage. Their resources and connections enable them to employ some of the best talent to help them reach their goals. This counsel knows the best practices, methods, research, and strategies to shortcut success.

Simply put, the successful have the opportunity to become even more successful. These outliers move to the front of the line faster.

Clarity

First class outliers don't have more talent or brains than others. What separates them is their clarity. This higher level of awareness enables them to see things differently.

For example, when the economy takes a downturn, the majority tends to panic. First class outliers often remain calm because they don't live paycheck to paycheck. They see the recession differently. This clarity helps them make intelligent decisions rather than impulse ones. Their clarity often leads to creativity and they find new opportunities in the so-called "crisis." Similarly, because these outliers tend to diversify their income, they spread out their risk and their reward.

First class clarity pays big dividends—even in difficult times.

Competence

Because first class outliers have clarity, they're also more aware of their strengths. They understand their competencies and deficiencies with razor sharp exactness. This knowledge helps them develop their strengths and delegate their weaknesses.

Comparatively speaking, other people don't know their unique skills. Because they're unclear, they end up repelling potential clients. No one buys their products or services because they come off as incompetent—and winners don't invest in incompetence.

First class outliers experience just the opposite. People invest in them because they've integrated the best strategies and systems. These tools allow them to execute at a much higher level and influence many more people.

First class competence frees you to be yourself and charge the fees that reflect your true value.

Confidence

First class outliers are confident. They know two important facts—their value in the marketplace and their ability to fulfill their promise.

As a result, they communicate belief—a critical component necessary for increasing influence, impact, and income. First class outliers know clients buy into them long before they buy into their product.

This confidence only earns them *temporary* trust. These outliers wisely cash in on confidence by over-delivering value. Even smarter yet, they draw clear lines between confidence and arrogance. Notice the difference:

- Arrogance says, "Watch me, I'm something special."
- Confidence says, "Trust me, I'll create results."
- Arrogance is focused on *self.*
- Confidence is focused on *serving.*

First class confidence positions you as a trustworthy source.

Discover the HOW: How to Join First Class Living

You've learned *what* first class living is and *why* you should join. Now it's time to discover *how* to join.

On an airplane, joining first class only costs you a little more cash. Yet a quick Google search revealed an interesting article titled, "How to Get an Upgrade to First Class."[82] The writer provided 18 creative "hacks" to join first class. Some hacks are helpful. Others feel just plain foolish. Read for yourself; there's a point to this process.

1. Buy an upgrade.
2. Become a frequent flier.
3. Check in at the airport kiosk.
4. Check in early.
5. Get bumped!
6. Find discounted tickets.
7. Plan long-term.
8. Book directly with the airline.
9. Buy a full fare coach ticket and ask for a first class seat.
10. Shop around.
11. Book with a travel agent.
12. Use a mileage broker.
13. Ask the ticket counter agent nicely.
14. If you were late because of a partner airline, make sure the airline is aware of that.
15. If you happen to be a travel agent, show your IATA or ARC ID.

16. Ask a flight attendant for an upgrade if you see a seat available.
17. Get to know the airline employees you deal with regularly.
18. Look the part.

If only becoming first class in life was as easy as

- looking the part (idea 18) or
- making friends with the airline employee (idea 17).

Unfortunately, it's not quite that simple. Joining first class *in life* costs a little bit more than cash. That said, I do agree with one of the strategies listed in the article—buy an upgrade (idea 1). According to the article:

> *"This is by far the easiest, most sure-fire way to get an upgrade. However, unless you fly often with the airline and have earned elite status, it's also the most expensive way to enjoy the perks of first class."*[83]

I believe the *only* way to join first class in life is through buying an upgrade. Of course, "buying" means more than cash in our context. Upgrades come by effort, not by income alone. Upgrading to first class requires an investment of your mind, body, and soul. In other words, it only comes with a holistic commitment. Let's take a closer look at each of the three required components.

Mind

Upgrading is a process, not an event. Both produce entirely different outcomes:

- Events motivate.
- Processes mature.

Joining first class is less about what you do and more about who you become. Author James Allen wrote a classic book more than 50 years ago called *As a Man Thinketh*. In it, he wrote:

> *"Every man is where he is by the law of his being; the thoughts which he has built into his character have brought him there, and in the arrangement of his life there is no element of chance, but all is the result of a law which cannot err."*

Allen titled his book after a proverb from my favorite book. The full proverb is:

> *"As a man thinketh, so is he."*[84]

Translation: your thoughts shape who you are. Because of this truth, I encourage my teams to make a note of what they're feeding themselves. I call it a Media Inventory and it involves a few simple questions:

- What are you consuming?
- Is this content helping you grow?
- Is this content designed to move you into first class?

If your media is quality content, an upgrade is inevitable. If not, you're going to remain stuck in coach class for longer than you'd like.

Body

I'm always amazed how often people segment their health from the rest of their lives. Obviously, your body goes wherever you do. If you're healthy, then you bring this into your work, play, and friendships. Similarly, if you're unhealthy, you bring this into every other area, too.

How you eat, how you exercise, and how you sleep directly affect your energy level. Low energy won't serve you because first class living and fatigue don't mix.

If you're unhealthy then you're due for an upgrade. If you don't listen to your body's signals, you'll eventually find yourself sidelined.

Soul

You're more than flesh and bones. You have unique worth and value. You have a distinct personality and destiny. You can develop this calling or deny it. Again, the choice is yours to make.

First class outliers make the commitment to reach their potential. This decision sinks deep below the surface and into their souls. It taps into their dreams and desires.

If you're willing to do some soul work, you're incredibly close to an upgrade. But if you're afraid to dig deep, you'll remain stuck, just above the surface.

Happy Landing

Although airplanes are built to soar, they're also made to land. This is true in the Higher Life Design context, too. So far you've seen the importance of the takeoff and flight phases. In the next chapter, you'll discover how to experience a happy landing.

Your goal isn't simply to get airborne. As breathtaking as they are, the friendly skies aren't your final stop. Higher Life Design Travelers have a loftier vision—one that involves arriving at their intended destination healthy, wealthy, and happy.

So, as the flight attendants say on every flight, "Ladies and gentlemen, please return to your seats. We're about to start the final descent to our intended destination."

Higher Life Design Traveler's Checklist

☐ I can achieve mastery because I've increased awareness by traveling through the Four Stages of Competence.

☐ I've invested 10,000 hours in my ideal area of expertise so I can become an outlier and experience a first class mindset.

☐ I take action every day so I can be a master in the art of living.

☐ I pursue first class connections so I can pursue a higher life.

☐ I employ first class counsel so I can achieve bigger goals.

☐ I experience first class clarity so I can remain solid in troubled times.

☐ I understand my value and skills so I can embody first class competence.

☐ I communicate first class confidence so I can earn my client's trust.

☐ I engage my mind, body, and soul intentionally so I can join first class living.

PART III

LANDING—
INTEGRATION

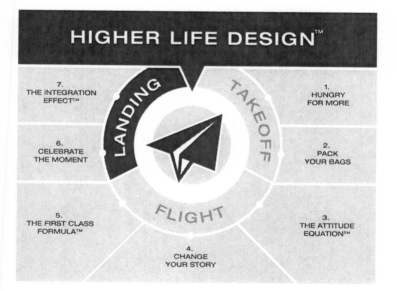

Step Six:
Celebrate the Moment

Deep presence creates wide futures

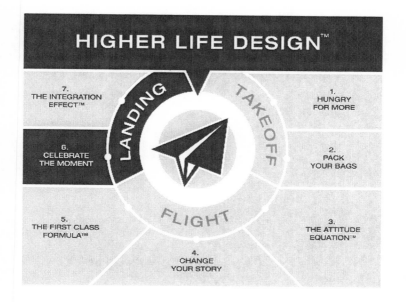

Growing up, I always had big dreams—traveling the world to exotic places, helping people with my acts of service, doing business internationally and learning a third language.

As I finished school and started working, I realized I was on a slow track toward my dreams. I felt frustrated and was constantly searching for a better way to live the life I really wanted.

After meeting Jefferson and following his guidance, I quickly realized that I, too, could lead a life of greatness and fulfill my dreams. With humility, he showed me how to recreate my story, regardless of my past.

I struggled as a single mom working two jobs and having little time to spend with my son. Living paycheck to paycheck frustrated me. Jefferson taught me how to be a better mom by spending more quality time with my son, getting out of debt, and traveling the world with the purpose of helping others to succeed.

I am forever grateful for leaders like Jefferson Santos, who has taught me how to Design a Higher Life!
— Irene H.

I'll never forget my first coaching call with Jefferson! Apparently, I was so quiet that he kept asking if I was still there. Each time, I assured him I was just taking notes. I knew I needed to transcribe every word possible.

His words captivated me. Jefferson taught me first class mindset as well as first class language skills. It changed EVERYTHING! People say to me all the time,

"You're such a wordsmith. You always have just the right thing to say and know HOW to say it!"

I still credit Jefferson for being the catalyst for change in my language skills. Because of Jefferson, my mindset changed, my language changed, and now my paycheck changed!

— **Nate R.**

A lthough I love flying, I love landing even more. Nothing compares to the feeling I get exploring a new part of the world. Just yesterday, I returned from a trip to Hong Kong, Thailand, and Singapore with my wife, Megan.

We enjoyed breathtaking views and sampled different kinds of food. I even tried durian. I made it through three bites before I realized it was too rich for my palate. Because we're expecting, Megan took a "pregnancy pass." Although it's called the "king of the fruits," the texture, smell, and taste were unlike anything I've ever tasted.

That same evening, we enjoyed a fresh seafood dinner that was much better than any we've tasted stateside. Nothing beats the real thing.

The next day—an ordinary Tuesday afternoon—we sat on a towering bluff eating mangoes with my buddy James Lee and our new friends. Nestled in Phuket, we took in sights and sounds too beautiful for words. Just do a Google search for "Kata Noi Beach" and you'll see what I mean.

Little Blue Signs with Big White Lettering

You should be here.

If we've hung out together, you've probably heard me say it. This phrase caught on so much, it's now tagged all over social media. Unless you know the meaning, though, you might not catch the message.

A few years ago, I was on a world tour with some friends.

The weather felt invigorating.

The food tasted wonderful.

The music sounded amazing.

Reflecting on the moment, one of the guys commented how it was absolutely perfect. We all agreed.

Then we heard something strange.

"No. It's not!"

The unwelcome comment came without warning, disrupting our ideal bliss. Did someone really disagree with our definition of utopia? Upon further investigation, evidently the commentator felt bummed that one of our friends couldn't make the trip. To his credit, when he pointed out our friend was absent, we all felt a little bummed.

Although we savored our experience, we also grieved the fact our friend didn't share it with us. Another quick thinker solved the problem by pulling out his phone to capture the moment on video. With everybody squeezing into the shot, someone shouted, "You should be here!"

That phrase explained our dilemma perfectly. Although blessed to experience this piece of international paradise, we all grieved the fact our friend missed out on the moment.

In spontaneous fashion, we joined in:

"You should be here."

Our chant grew louder:

"You Should Be Here!"

"YOU SHOULD BE HERE!!!"

The rest is—as they say—history.

Years later, we've printed tens of thousands of these small blue signs with big white lettering. Look online and you'll find people holding these signs while sky-diving, jet-skiing, bungee jumping, parasailing, scuba diving, and four-wheeling.

You'll see these signs in oceans, on top of mountains, and under waterfalls. You'll locate them on hunting excursions, at major sporting events, and inside schools being built on our VolunTourism trips.

The message is simple: *YOU SHOULD BE HERE!*

But the meaning is multifaceted:

- *Be Here*—seeing new sights.
- *Be Here*—tasting new foods.
- *Be Here*—experiencing different countries and cultures.

Higher Life Design Travelers don't miss the moment. They know time doesn't wait to show up. Time marches on—with or without you.

Where are You, Anyway?

Some people get the false impression I travel every day. Let me clear up any confusion. I don't—at least not literally.

That said, I do feel like every day in my life is an adventure. I achieve this mindset with a rather simple strategy—choosing to be fully present by *celebrating the moment*. Although it sounds easy, it's rather difficult to do.

A while ago, I discovered an interesting phenomenon. I noticed many people appear to be physically present at dinner tables, coffee chats, and sporting events. Upon further investigation, their minds seemed to be elsewhere.

Unfortunately, your loved ones sense it when you miss the moment. They feel your absence even if you think you're great at hiding it. When you're missing the moment, you're missing out on the Higher Life Design.

Before we go any further, let's first remove any guilt. I don't think anyone wakes up and says, "Today I'm going to choose to be absent from my life. I'm going to intentionally miss out on my most important moments."

No, I think it's much more subtle than that.

Four Temptations and Four Tactics

Like everyone else, Higher Life Design Travelers feel the same four temptations that lure them to miss the moment. However, they combat these temptations with four tactics that help them celebrate the moment instead. Here's a look at each.

Temptation	Tactic
1. Coping with Pain	1. Celebrate Choice
2. Abusing Technology	2. Celebrate Breaks
3. Excessive Busyness	3. Celebrate Rest
4. Blind Conformity	4. Celebrate Craziness

Temptation 1: Coping with Pain

The last time I checked, avoiding pain seemed like a fairly smart goal. As a rule, I'm not someone who particularly enjoys pain. I think you'd probably agree.

As humans, we take great measures to insulate and isolate ourselves from pain. Most new parents begin employing this strategy the moment their child arrives in this world. I know we did.

I remember driving our baby boy home from the hospital. We buckled Harrison in a cage of comfort—a car seat. Even though this miniature sanctuary remained firmly fixed between four walls of airbags, 20 miles per hour still felt too fast. Privileged to be his daddy, I vowed to keep pain out of the vehicle—no matter the cost.

I only succeeded for a short time, of course. As we all know, pain is part of life. Just ask a child after he gets a shot at the doctor's office. Pain eventually rips into our awareness.

Pain can be good, though. Anyone who exercises vigorously knows what I'm talking about. True results only come with pain. This applies in academics as well as relationships. Excellence in anything takes discipline and discipline requires pain.

One of my friends said it like this, "Pain is inevitable. Misery is a choice."

Marketers tend to disagree. They create hot-selling products that thrive on the illusion of eradicating pain. Although this sounds promising, it's simply impossible. People see through this. So instead, many simply settle for numbing their pain instead. One popular strategy of choice is called disassociation.[85]

This psychological term refers to people intentionally missing the moment by detaching themselves mentally. According to psychological experts, disassociation is a defense mechanism that helps minimize or tolerate stress—including boredom or conflict.[86] Simply put, people dissociate from situations because the present moment is too painful.

This strategy is often used where people spend the most time—at work. Disassociation allows these disengaged people to "check out" mentally. It helps them pass the time faster and escape the pain of working in a job they hate.

Disengaged employees are more common than you might think. The Gallup Organization regularly surveys employees in the United States and around the world.[87] They've discovered some shocking statistics about engagement in the workplace.

The most recent findings for United States workers may surprise you.[88] (Many other countries reveal an even dimmer reality.[89]) Employees fall into 3 categories—not engaged, actively disengaged, and engaged. Here's how it breaks down:

Not Engaged
Fifty-two percent of the US working population is not engaged. These people do just enough to get a paycheck. Merely going through the motions, if they could leave their jobs they would. They live and work from half of a heart.

Actively Disengaged
Eighteen percent of the US working population is actively disengaged. These people take calculated, strategic steps to steal from their employer, spread lies about co-workers, and create disunity in their work environment. They communicate their disengagement through unproductive actions. They sabotage themselves and those around them. They're not bad people, but they're "stuck" people acting negatively. They live and work from a broken heart.

Engaged

Thirty percent of the US working population is engaged. This small segment takes responsibility and ownership for their assignments. They realize their work is an extension of themselves and because they're on fire, so is everything they touch. They live and work from a full heart.

Referencing this Gallup research, 70 percent of US workers are not engaged or actively disengaged. This classification carries a financial cost "up to $550 billion annually in lost productivity."[90]

Tactic 1: Celebrate Choice

You have options and understanding these options helps you get closer to celebrating the moment.

Life is too short to spend tens of thousands of hours in misery. Scraping by and holding out for the weekends is no way to live. Life is too short *not* to make the maximum contribution with the gifts and abilities entrusted to you.

Steve Jobs understood this brevity. It served as a filter for choices, including his employment choices. He said:

> "When I was 17, I read a quote that went something like: 'If you live each day as if it was your last, someday you'll most certainly be right.' It made an impression on me, and since then, for the past 33 years, I have looked in the mirror every morning and asked myself: 'If today were the last day of my life, would I want to do what I am about to do today?' And whenever the answer has

been 'No' for too many days in a row, I know I need to change something."[91]

Sounds too easy, right?

Maybe not.

If you're in a job you hate, you can leave. The company I'm part of helps people make a sensible transition. It affords them increased freedom, additional finances, and greater fulfillment. Thousands of people create another income stream *while* they work their day jobs. When they feel the time is right, they make the shift to do what they love on a full-time basis. Ironically, many of my team members are so successful in their businesses, they only need to work their dream job on a part-time basis.

It's a great time to be alive and your chances for success are far greater today than at any other time in human history. According to Darren Hardy, who co-founded an Internet company in early 2000, "Your chance at entrepreneurial success is 564 times greater than just 13 years ago."[92]

He explained why. "We raised several million dollars to get started. Building the website, the software to run it and servers to deliver it cost nearly $1 million. Today that website could be built for less than $5,000. We spent the other millions to hire experienced tech talent (we paid a high price because of limited supply) and on marketing in the days before Google AdWords, Facebook, Twitter, Pinterest, etc."

Fight the temptation to cope with pain by dissociating. You do have choices. Many of these include the benefit of celebrating the moment rather than missing it. Your family and friends will thank you for choosing wisely.

Temptation 2: Abusing Technology

Get ready for the biggest understatement of the century.

Times have changed.

Every day, the average person produces six newspapers' worth of information compared with just two and a half pages' worth 24 years ago—nearly a 200-fold increase. This number doesn't compare to the amount of information we receive on a daily basis—more than 174 newspapers' worth.[93]

The amount of data produced through social media alone is staggering:

- People and brands on Twitter send more than 340 million tweets a day.
- People send more than 144.8 billion email messages in a day.
- People on Facebook share more than 684,000 bits of content a day.
- People upload 72 hours (259,200 seconds) of new video to YouTube a minute.
- Google receives more than 2 million search queries a minute.
- Apple provides around 47,000 app downloads a minute.
- Brands receive more than 34,000 Facebook "likes" a minute.
- Tumblr blog owners publish 27,000 new posts a minute.

- Instagram photographers share 3,600 new photos a minute.
- Flickr photographers upload 3,125 new photos a minute.
- People perform more than 2,000 Foursquare check-ins a minute.
- Individuals and organizations launch 571 new websites a minute.
- WordPress bloggers publish close to 350 new blog posts a minute.[94]

Get ready for the second biggest understatement of the century.

With 300 times more bits of information than grains of sand on the earth, it's fairly easy to miss the moment.

Tactic 2: Celebrate Breaks

Unless you break from the noise often exacerbated by technology, you won't be able to celebrate the moment.

Hundreds of years ago, Blaise Pascal saw this tendency even before DVRs, movies, or electricity. He wrote, "All of man's difficulties are caused by his inability to sit quietly in a room by himself."[95]

You might be thinking, "Really? All of my difficulties result from a lack of reflection caused by an addiction to the noise?" Pascal thought so.

Noise prevents you from thinking deeply about yourself, others, and life's most important question. Centuries after

Pascal, Thomas Edison observed this trend in his generation. He said, "Five percent of the people think; ten percent of the people think they think; and the other eighty-five percent would rather die than think."[96]

On the surface, technology seems innocent enough. Sure, it fills your life with "noise," but it also provides you with amusement. That's not bad until you realize the etymology of the word *amusement*.

amusement

> *a* = not
>
> *muse* = think

According to its origins, amusement literally means to "not think." Amusement is designed "to distract and divert" you from the present moment. Though some technology can be helpful, it largely exists for amusement. If you think technology doesn't threaten your ability to celebrate the moment, think again.

Thanks to an insightful post by Mark Sisson, author of *The Primal Blueprint*, I learned the true magnitude of this threat:

> *"According to a recent survey of people in 65 countries, 73.4% of people own a smartphone. Those with smartphones check them an average of 110 times per day, which amounts to every five or six minutes spread out over a twelve hour period. Another study found a slightly higher frequency—150 times per day."*[97]

While results vary, people addicted to technology miss the moment. Many also suffer from these physiological symptoms:

- **Text Neck:** Smartphones cause you to jut your head forward and bend your neck, placing a huge amount of stress on your vertebrae.

- **Gameboy Back:** Frequent "gaming" on smartphones and other handheld devices places thoracic spines in flexion for extended periods of time. Growing kids, whose skeletal systems are still developing, are most vulnerable.

- **Text Claw:** Sending texts a hundred times a day and writing entire emails using your thumbs overuses tendons in your hands.

- **Sleep Texting:** Many people sleep next to their phones and answer incoming text messages while half asleep. Similar to talking while intoxicated, they don't remember what they said when morning comes. Besides disrupting your sleep, this practice makes you miss the moment no matter how awake you "feel."

- **Phantom Phone Vibration:** Research reveals people experiencing the sensation of their phones vibrating in their pockets or purses even when they are not. Though not dangerous, this increasing phenomenon proves how technology now disrupts our thinking, even when it's turned off.

- **Internet Addiction:** As stated in *Forbes* magazine, the latest edition of the Diagnostic and Statistical Manual of Mental Disorders (DSM-5) now includes Internet Addiction Disorder.[98] Additional studies found in the Harvard Business Review reveal that receiving Facebook "Likes" gives a hit of dopamine to your reward system.[99] Because of growing research, the healthcare industry is now acknowledging the tendency for people to miss the moment. As a result, they've responded by creating legitimate treatment, such as a Pennsylvania hospital offering an IAD (Internet Addiction Disorder) inpatient program.

- **Depression:** The more frequently you use social media or check your phone, the more likely you are to report feeling sad, depressed, and lonely. A recent study in young adults showed that Facebook use predicts declines in subjective well-being, while "direct" contact with people does not. Clinicians have referred to this as "Facebook depression."[100]

Please don't misunderstand me. I don't believe technology is the enemy. I believe it's simply a tool. However, an addiction to technology sabotages many would be Higher Life Design Travelers. Fight the temptation of technology abuse by scheduling breaks and celebrating the moment instead.

Temptation 3: Excessive Busyness

You probably know people who are *money* rich and *time* poor. I know I do. They have possessions, but no time to enjoy them. These people respond to the universal greeting, "How are you?" with a boast cloaked in a subtle complaint.

- "I'm *busy*."
- "I'm *super* busy."
- "I'm *crazy* busy."

When did this response become a badge of honor? Imagine if you heard the opposite reply—one often said by Higher Life Design Travelers.

- "I'm *relaxed*."
- "I'm *super* relaxed."
- "I'm *crazy* relaxed."

This type of response produces questions, confusion, and perhaps even a little jealousy. When you first hear it, you might be tempted to think these people are clueless, unimportant, or perhaps even a little strange. Maybe they are strange, but is that a bad thing?

Pascal, the seventeenth century Renaissance man, commented on this "crazy busy" pace with amazing clarity.

I know what you might be thinking: what does some guy who's been dead for almost 400 years know about busyness? They didn't have electricity, video games, or the Internet then.

That's what I thought until I read his words. It's eerie— almost like he peeked ahead 400 years into the future. Other than a few archaic words, notice the relevancy of his thoughts:

> *"The only thing that consoles us for our miseries is distraction, yet that is the greatest of our wretchedness.*

Because that is what mainly prevents us from thinking about ourselves.... Without it we should be bored, and boredom would force us to search for a firmer way out, but distraction entertains us and leads us imperceptibly to death."[101]

It sounds like Pascal ran into a few busy people in his day. Let me rephrase his words in our vernacular:

You stay busy to avoid the intense ache for fulfillment. Distraction enables you to mask the truth. If you welcomed boredom instead, you'd be forced to do the deeper work and you'd end up experiencing true fulfillment instead.

Maybe the creators of *The Matrix* film should pay some of their royalties back to Pascal. He exposed the idea—that busyness distracts us from the truth—centuries before the Wachowskis did. Maybe that's why *The Matrix* resonated with so many people?

In that movie, Agent Smith commented on how the Matrix successfully distracted the human race. "Have you ever stood and stared at it; marveled at its beauty, its genius?" he asked. "Billions of people just living out their lives, oblivious."[102]

Because humans were distracted with busy lives, they didn't notice the truth—that machines were using them as glorified batteries. The Matrix—a control mechanism created by machines—served as a way of harvesting human's electrical energy to power other machines. As long as humans kept running from activity to activity, they remained oblivious to their own impending destruction.

This film was classified as science fiction—mere fantasy. Maybe movie experts need to rethink this one. It sounds a bit like real life to me.

Tactic 3: Celebrate Rest

I don't *really* think machines are using your electrical energy for power. However, I do believe without adequate rest, you'll quickly *feel* like a machine. Remember—you're a human being, not a human doing.

Busy people miss the moment. You need rest. Without it, you'll burn out and dry up. You need time to withdraw, replenish, and recover like all Higher Life Design Travelers do.

Any time I wonder if I'm too busy, I probably am. At those times, I stop long enough to take a Personal Rest Quiz (PRQ). Although it only takes two minutes to complete, it helps me get centered rather quickly.

I encourage you take your own PRQ. Be advised: it only works when you provide honest answers.

I don't know about you, but when I take this PRQ, I feel the need to create a "Sometimes" column. If you do, too, just ignore those feelings. Don't give in to the temptation. This tactic of celebrating rest only works when you commit to clarity, and clarity only comes with honesty.

Personal Rest Quiz	*Yes*	*No*
1. I'm sleeping long enough and often enough.		
2. I feel energized.		
3. I've built margins into my life.		
4. I am a person who is present.		
5. I take time to care for myself physically, spiritually, and emotionally.		
6. I notice sights, smells, sounds, and people throughout the day.		
7. I enjoy feasting and laughing with loved ones.		
8. In the last week, I enjoyed the outdoors without the need for scheduled activity.		
9. In the last week, I took a break and unplugged from appointments.		
10. In the last week, I remembered to breathe slowly and deeply.		

How many checks did you make in the "No" column? If more than one, you're probably too busy. True presence only comes when you're at peace. Busyness may appear productive, but at what cost? Stress, burnout, and depression seem like a high price to pay.

Fight the temptation of technology abuse and general busyness by scheduling breaks and celebrating the moment instead.

Temptation 4: Blind Conformity

The final temptation that calls you to miss the moment is actually quite boring. Ironically, that's the problem. Conformity tempts you to be predictable and uneventful—to play it safe by simply blending in with those around you. Unfortunately, when you're comfortable, you're coasting, and when you're coasting, you've increased your chances of missing the moment. When you're stuck in a rut, you go through life sleepwalking. In that state, there's no need for creativity or innovation.

Contrast this with Higher Life Design Travelers. They know growth only occurs on the edges. That's why they live life on the edge. They're always growing and emerging. Forget fitting in the mold. They broke the mold! These elite travelers supersede status quo by celebrating their craziness.

Tactic 4: Celebrate Craziness

If you look at the world long enough, you'll probably see opportunities and injustices. Most people see this, but nonconformists do something crazy. They take action.

We applaud their initiative and congratulate their courage. While the masses sit sidelined by silence, nonconformists stand up and shout out. Throughout history, they not only cursed the darkness, they also lit a candle. They not only told us what they're against, but they've also showed us what they're for.

Sink your teeth into 60 seconds of nonconformist attitude via Apple's "Think Different" advertising campaign. Debuted on September 28, 1997, it marked the beginning of Apple's Renaissance period and was credited with setting the company back on course. I'll warn you—it's convicting. You can check out the video free online. I've included the text here.[103]

> *"Here's to the crazy ones, the misfits, the rebels, the trouble-makers, the round pegs in the square holes, the ones who see things differently. They're not fond of rules and they have no respect for the status-quo. You can quote them, disagree with them, glorify, or vilify them. About the only thing you can't do is ignore them because they change things. They push the human race forward and, while some may see them as the crazy ones, we see genius, because the people who are crazy enough to think they can change the world are the ones who do."[104]*

The one-minute commercial featured black-and-white footage of 17 iconic twentieth century personalities who were nonconformists.

Albert Einstein	Maria Callas
Bob Dylan	Mahatma Gandhi
Martin Luther King, Jr.	Amelia Earhart
Richard Branson	Alfred Hitchcock
John Lennon (with Yoko Ono)	Martha Graham
Buckminster Fuller	Jim Henson (with Kermit
Thomas Edison	the Frog)
Muhammad Ali	Frank Lloyd Wright
Ted Turner	Pablo Picasso

Steve Jobs, the co-founder of Apple, typified this "crazy" clan. His unconventional actions simply flowed from his unconventional thinking, as captured in a PBS documentary titled *One Last Thing*.[105] In the documentary, he communicated a little more about his craziness:

> *"When you grow up you tend to get told the world is the way it is and you're life is just to live your life inside the world. Try not to bash into the walls too much. Try to have a nice family, have fun, save a little money. That's a very limited life. Life can be much broader once you discover one simple fact: Everything around you that you call life was made up by people that were no smarter than you and you can change it, you can influence it, you can build your own things that other people can use. Once you learn that, you'll never be the same again."*

Does he sound a little crazy? Maybe, but I don't think that's such a bad thing.

If you want to get what no one is getting, you need to do what no one is doing. Rather than avoiding craziness, you need to start celebrating it.

Deep Presence Creates Wide Futures

Experiencing the moment—rather than missing the moment—has its advantages. For starters, it allows your family and friends to feel your presence. Further, it prevents physiological symptoms that will slow you down.

However, beyond all the benefits we explored in this chapter, the greatest is that deep presence creates wide futures. Alert and engaged people maximize the moment at a much higher level than those who simply coast through life.

Let me congratulate you because:

You're *not* one of those sleepwalking through life.

You've journeyed through the first six steps of the Higher Life Design.

You're now ready to take the final step—The Integration Effect.

Higher Life Design Traveler's Checklist

☐ I stretched as a person because I explored a new part of the world in the last month.

☐ I make every day an adventure by celebrating the present.

☐ I use the four tactics to help me fight the four temptations that lure me to miss the moment.

☐ I refrain from disassociating as a strategy for coping with my pain.

☐ I schedule breaks from technology so I actually live life instead of simply watching it.

☐ I balance my use of technology so I avoid harmful physiological symptoms.

☐ I don't allow amusement to distract and divert me from the present.

☐ I take the Personal Rest Quiz (PRQ) weekly so I can remain balanced instead of busy.

☐ I continue to grow so I remain creative and innovative.

☐ I do what others don't do so I can get what others don't get.

Step Seven:
The Integration Effect

Healthy fruits come from strong roots

No one has impacted my life more positively than Jefferson Santos. Having been to numerous other seminars, I can honestly say there is no one else I wish to model more.

Before following Jefferson's success principles, I had a good job but I was working nearly 100 hours a week. No matter how many hours I worked, I couldn't chip away at the hundreds of thousands of dollars of debt I incurred.

Now, three years later, my net worth is $400,000, my marriage is incredible, and I've taken a vacation every month this year. Jefferson helped me open the door to a level of happiness I didn't think was possible. As I continue to learn, I'm now teaching these principles to my children so our family can be more successful for generations.

—**Will J.**

I've struggled with business and financial challenges, but I always wanted to travel the world and give my family a good quality life. I worked hard, but clearly I was going nowhere.

When I met Jefferson, he was like a breath of fresh air. His energy and enthusiasm attracted me to what he was doing. Clearly he was going somewhere.

He gave me the courage to chase after my dreams by doing what he taught. Since then, I have designed my ideal life through his Higher Life Design.

Thank you, Jefferson!

—**Soojay D.**

I like sprouts.

Not the kind you eat, but the kind you plant; not in the ground, but in your life. I'm not a gardener, so the sprouts I like are symbolic, not literal. In my mind, sprouts are small initiatives that contain big potential.

When I teach my teams, I tell them to pay attention to their sprouts. It's now become one of the Higher Life Design habits. Here's why.

Oftentimes while reflecting upon your day, it's easy to wonder what you've accomplished. Sure, you're busy—we all are. The more important question is, were you productive?

Very rarely do you ever have a day where you plant an entire "tree." In your context, planting a "tree" might be closing a deal, finishing a project, or landing a new client. These big payoffs probably only come along occasionally.

More often, your day is sprinkled with "sprouts" instead of "trees." Your "sprouts" might be choosing a healthful snack, following up on a lead, or reading a chapter in a personal growth book.

Sprouts are so small that most people overlook them. Unfortunately, when you overlook your sprouts they simply die. Nobody waters things they don't notice and, without proper attention and effort, sprouts just shrivel up.

If you're not looking for sprouts, you'll miss them. You'll walk right past them or, heaven forbid, you'll unintentionally step on them—not cool. The only thing that results from undeveloped sprouts is regret.

However, if you do see your sprouts and if you do exert proper attention and effort to growing them, they'll turn into something worth talking about. Think about it—every tree was once a small sprout. As the fourteenth century proverb teaches, "Great oaks from little acorns grow."[106]

When you place an acorn in the ground, it grows into a small sprout that sends out a powerful signal to the surrounding soil. It attracts everything it needs to grow and thrive. Miraculously, it grows, increasing in size and strength.

This same acorn—now a mighty oak—produces other acorns. The average oak tree produces 70,000–150,000 acorns per year.[107] During the tree's entire life, it produces around 13.5 million acorns.[108] This staggering number doesn't even account for the acorns that will be produced by the trees that sprout from this tree's acorns, or from the trees that sprout from those trees' acorns, and so on.

The next time you see a sprout in your life, realize the potential of 13.5 million other sprouts coming from that single one.

The Integration Effect

It sounds basic, but giving your sprouts the proper attention and effort they need to grow is both an art and a science. I've developed a process called The Integration Effect to make it easier. Applying this process will help you see how small initiatives can produce big results. Just remember the word S.P.R.O.U.T.S. and you'll be well on your way.

The Integration Effect

S = **S**top

P = **P**onder

R = **R**ecord

O = **O**ptimize

U = **U**tilize

T = **T**rack

S = **S**hare

Let's dig into each of these actions one at a time.

S = *Stop*

To see your sprouts, you're going to have to do something you might not want to do. You're going to have to STOP.

Experts tell us we are distracted every three minutes. That sounds bad, but it gets worse. It takes 11 minutes to regain concentration. This means for most people, their entire day is one big distraction.

You struggle stopping because it feels so unproductive. Here's the irony—the most productive people build in "stop" time. Former CEO of GE Jack Welch scheduled an hour a day for "looking out the window time." And despite the intense demands placed on him when he served as leader of Microsoft, Bill Gates blocked off two "think weeks" every year. Both of these former high-powered CEOs understood unless they stopped, they wouldn't be able to go.

Stopping feels odd because we've been taught to mistake

- activity for accomplishment
- movement for achievement
- rushing for results

Increasing activity without stopping only results in a diminishing effect. It decreases energy reserves and breaks down mental focus. In this state, the same amount of effort yields much lower levels of productivity.

Remember—to see your sprouts you're going to have to stop.

P = Ponder

One of my friends says, "Pay attention to what you pay attention to." In other words, there's a rhyme and reason for the subjects on which you focus. Tap into that truth by digging deeper. Ask yourself:

- Why do I enjoy certain topics?
- Why do I engage in specific activities?
- Why do I come back to particular places?

You'll discover these answers when you stop long enough to reflect. One of my mentors, John C. Maxwell, designated a time and a place to ponder.

Time

Maxwell pauses to ponder regularly. It's one the five activities he does on a daily basis. His other four activities are reading, filing, asking questions, and writing. Despite a daily ritual of pondering, Maxwell also blocks off a large segment of time between Christmas Day and New Year's Day to engage in a comprehensive reflection process. Through this process, he's able to identify his sprouts and make intelligent decisions about the upcoming year. He intentionally invests more time on his sprouts and less time on his weeds. This distinction makes a difference.

Place

Let's face it—life often becomes hectic. For this reason, I suggest establishing a place of solitude. This space will serve as your "distraction free zone." Maxwell also devoted a place to think. He calls it his "thinking chair." Logically, whenever Maxwell sits in that particular chair, he's naturally primed to ponder.

Remember—pondering your sprouts requires a devoted time and place.

R = Record

Earl Nightingale said, "Ideas are like slippery fish; they have a peculiar knack for getting away from us unless we gaffe them on the point of a pencil."[109]

Nightingale knew something important—ideas visit us only momentarily. Ideas always start out as sprouts, and the best ones grow strong over time. Unfortunately, if we fail to record them, they'll die before they have time to take root.

With today's technology, there's really no longer an excuse to let them fade. Most smart phones have voice recording capability, and the latest apps—such as Evernote or Springpad—will help you capture and archive these sprouts. Whichever tools you use, it's important to have a system you use consistently to capture and process your thoughts. Many people find David Allen's *Getting Things Done* system to be useful. Find the tools and systems that work and keep at it. By capturing your thoughts, you'll an abundant supply of potential. Best of all, you'll know where to locate it.

Remember—recording your sprouts allows them to grow bigger.

O = Optimize

Today you have more information coming at you than at any other time in history. While serving as the CEO of Google, Eric Schmidt made an interesting observation. He said, "All the information ever created in human history up to 2003 is now created every two days."[110]

This amount of information overload today will overwhelm anyone. This truth motivated Darren Hardy, publisher of *Success* magazine, to say managing distractions is the number one differentiator that separates successful people from unsuccessful people. He further explained that the most important skill of the twenty-first century is learning to control your attention.

We live in an age of distraction and the next generation is getting distracted much earlier in life. The average 13-17 year-old exchanges 4,000 text messages per month, or one every six minutes.[111]

To be honest, adults aren't any better. One study reported that office workers checked their email as often as 40 times per hour.[112] If you're not careful, all these distractions will prevent you from seeing your sprouts and from doing anything significant with those sprouts.

The truth is, everyone likes to look busy and some people even make a career out of it. Bustling around and accomplishing very little is simply "active non-action." It doesn't serve you or your team.

Science proves the mind can only focus on one thing at a time. Multi-tasking may seem attractive, but in reality it's only a myth. James Johnston, research psychologist at NASA, reported, "When you 'multi-task' it's inevitable that each individual task may be slower and of lower quality."[113]

I get it.

You probably do too. Even so, many of us still feel the need to multi-task. The myth promises you the illusion of achieving more, but does the promise transfer to reality? A recent report showed workers distracted by email and phone calls suffer a fall in IQ more than twice that found in marijuana smokers.[114]

According to Peter Bregman in *Harvard Business Review,* "Doing several things at once is a trick we play on ourselves, thinking we're getting more done. In reality, our productivity goes down by as much as 40 percent. We don't actually multitask. We switch-task, rapidly shifting from one thing to another, interrupting ourselves unproductively, and losing time in the process."[115]

Though you might be able to walk and chew gum at the same time, you cannot perform two cognitive tasks simultaneously. When you try, your limited brain resources must be reallocated. This repeated "switch-tasking" produces stress, not to mention impaired productivity. Higher Life Design Travelers recognize multi-tasking prevents them from integrating their sprouts effectively.

Remember—maintaining a single focus optimizes your efforts and enables your sprouts to thrive.

U = Utilize

While most people only sit and speculate, Higher Life Design Travelers take action and invest time, money, and effort in growing their sprouts. This bias toward action produces bigger results, faster.

If you look closely, you'll see all kinds of helpful resources and relationships all around you. I've been honored and humbled by those willing to support my sprouts. Some of this support came through strategic masterminds and others through incredible training videos. The point is, we're all resourced if we just know where to look.

Remember—utilizing every resource and relationship will grow yourself and your sprouts.

T = Track

Nobody plants a seed and then digs it up the next day out of frustration by the lack of growth. The law of gender states that everything has its own gestation or incubation period.[116] We know it takes nine months to create a baby. We can also calculate the incubation period of trees, plants, fruits, vegetables, and flowers. Similarly, your sprouts require a certain period before you'll see rapid growth. Don't get frustrated if you don't see results instantly.

Back when you were a kid, perhaps someone regularly measured your height. Maybe they had you stand against a wall and chart your growth with a pencil mark. You probably didn't feel yourself growing, but tracking your growth helped remove any doubt. Those pencil marks provided all the proof you needed.

Remember—tracking your sprouts helps you stay positive and encouraged.

S = *Share*

Sprouts don't stay small forever. They grow! Even better—they produce fruit. You've worked hard and you need to take time to enjoy the "fruit" of your labor—literally. Besides nourishing you, this fruit also nourishes those around you. Because you've received, you're now able to give more to others.

I've experienced this firsthand. I've been blessed to learn from some of the best experts in the industry. After investing time with them, I feel incredibly full of wisdom, energy, and passion. I could spend all this "fruit" on myself, but I choose to give it away. By sharing this fruit with my team, I'm able to internalize it in a greater way while simultaneously helping others grow.

Remember—sharing your fruit helps you integrate success on a much deeper level.

Higher Life Design Traveler's Checklist

☐ I pay attention to my sprouts so I don't miss the potential around me and within me.

☐ I remember small initiatives can produce big results.

☐ I STOP long enough to see my spouts so I can exert time and energy to see them grow.

☐ I designate a time and place to PONDER my spouts so I can reap an abundant reward.

☐ I've developed a system to RECORD my spouts so they don't slip away from me.

☐ I maintain a single focus and OPTIMIZE my efforts so my sprouts continue to thrive.

☐ I UTILIZE every resource and relationship so I can grow myself and my sprouts.

☐ I TRACK my sprout growth to help me stay positive and encouraged.

☐ I SHARE my fruit so I integrate success on a much deeper level.

Conclusion: The Higher Life Design Manifesto

Welcome to your intended destination

Jefferson taught me we can all reinvent, restart and re-launch our lives. He demonstrates no matter how difficult life gets and no matter what the past has been, anyone can begin again. Truly, we are all capable making the Higher Life Design a reality.
— **Erwin M.**

W hen you decided to read this book, you decided to join me on a journey. Together we explored a new way of thinking called the Higher Life Design. We moved through three different phases:

PART I: TAKEOFF—*Expectation*
PART II: FLIGHT—*Preparation*
PART III: LANDING—*Integration*

Within these three phases, we encountered the seven steps that compose the Higher Life Design:

Step One: Hungry for More
> Your influence increases in direct proportion to your appetite

Step Two: Pack Your Bags
> The right packing eliminates the wrong baggage

Step Three: The Attitude Equation
> Higher Altitude = Better Attitude

Step Four: Change Your Story
> To change yourself, you must first change your story

Step Five: The First Class Formula
> Never second guess the power of first class

Step Six: Celebrate the Moment
> Deep presence creates wide futures

Step Seven: The Integration Effect
> Healthy fruits come from strong roots

It's easy to forget The Higher Life Design is more than simply a new way of *thinking*. It's truly a new way of *living*. The power of the paradigm is found in application. Our growing tribe would agree. All over the world, brave souls are making a bold move: they're exchanging average for extraordinary and dull for indescribable.

Higher Life Design Travelers share a common belief—it is possible to arrive at your intended destination healthy, wealthy, and happy. Think of this belief as a snapshot of how you see the world.

Some might call this snapshot a manifesto.

I must prepare you—manifestos are powerful. Though they are short declarations of intent, they communicate values and at times they even invoke action. A manifesto is, after all, designed to clarify what we want to manifest in our lives. After reading it, you might just decide to join us—permanently.

I'm not saying that's a bad idea. In fact, I'd call it a rather brilliant one.

Welcome to our manifesto.

THE HIGHER LIFE
DESIGN MANIFESTO

(For Kim Eaton 1958-2008)

Buckle up, ladies and gentlemen. It's going to get a little bumpy. To meet the better version of you, you're going to have to go on a journey.

Many people punch the clock, go through the motions, and wear the mask. Their performance might earn them the promotion, the pension, or even the gold watch, but this charade costs them their hopes, their dreams, and even their hearts.

Make no mistake, you were destined for more than simply surviving. Remember, you were created for more than putting food on the table.

An unfulfilled life is an empty one, and the last time I checked, you're not coming back. You've got one shot to discover your voice, find your passion, and make your mark. Rationalize and speculate, but don't be late, because this is your moment.

Chock full of expectations, you're now prepared for takeoff. Your Higher Life Design is poised—waiting for you to show up. Our tribe is growing steadily, but we're still missing a key traveler. Our appetite for influence increases daily, but we need you with us because you're hungry for more.

You've done the deeper work and packed your bags accordingly. You've refused to let anyone or anything weigh you down or hold you back. Because you've prepared, you're now ready to fly further and faster. You've never dreamed small and now is no time to start. The altitude of your vision creates a contagious attitude for all who encounter it.

You don't get what you want; you get what you argue for. Therefore, it's time to change yourself, by first changing your story.

Never second guess the power of first class. Your upgrade is inevitable and a long time coming. It's time to land and integrate this Higher Life Design.

On the other side of this journey, you live as someone fully present. You embrace this new future defined by innovation and exploration.

Taste the fruit from your life. Enjoy this health, wealth, and happiness. Share your success with those around you. They are blessed by your efforts. Celebrate the moment. You've arrived at your intended destination:

the Higher Life Design.

Appendix

I dedicated the Higher Life Design Manifesto to a special teammate I met in 2001. Although twenty years older than me, Kim Eaton was always young at heart. She started her journey sitting shyly in the back row at our company event. But as time marched on, she found her way to the front row and eventually onto the main stage. It's here where Kim found her voice and communicated the new vision for her life. We—the audience—heard her intended destination defined by health, wealth, and happiness.

Although she's no longer with us, her impact will never fade. In my mind, she exemplifies a Higher Life Design Traveller. Before Kim passed she wrote me a letter that documents her journey of transformation. I hope her words spur you on in your own journey toward the Higher Life Design.

Trusting and Receiving
By Kim Eaton

I grew up in Queens, New York, one of the five boroughs that make up New York City. My father was a career Marine, a twenty-year man. My mother was a math genius, a wit, a strategist, and an artist. But being an African-American woman born over 70 years ago, that meant she was whatever mainstream America would let her be.

A domestic, a department store salesperson, and a data entry clerk in a milk factory. No job she ever had in the marketplace, came close to revealing who she was, or what she could have been. No job she ever had, gave her the ability to give her children all that she wanted them to have. Not even a ten-cent ice cream cone.

When I was eight-years-old, the "Mr. Softee" ice cream truck would come by in the summer afternoons. An ice cream cone was ten-cents, but ten-cents was more money than my mother had.

On one particular day, I saw one of my friends with an ice cream cone. I asked her for a lick. Unbeknownst to me, my mother saw me. She ran up to me and yelled that I should never do that again. She told me I was "begging" and I should never ask anyone for anything she couldn't give me.

My eight-year-old spirit was profoundly affected, because I had no way of understanding why a simple request for a lick of vanilla ice cream could cause such anger. My mother was embarrassed her daughter had to go asking for ice cream she couldn't afford to buy.

I had no way of understanding how much she must have hurt. Despite all her effort every week, she still couldn't afford the simple gift of an ice cream cone.

All I knew was that I asked for help, and it caused intense anger. In my mind, I translated that into several limiting beliefs I carried with me my entire life:

Never ask for help.

Never show weakness.

Never let anyone know I need help.

Never.

Several years ago, I started in a travel company trying to build a life where I could finally find the joy that had eluded me all of my years. One of the 'major players' in my company is a young man named Jefferson Santos. Young enough to be my son, he is wise beyond his years, articulate, energetic, and a visionary. Still, he was not someone I ever saw as a mentor for me.

I saw no common threads running through our lives. Not the same age group, racial group, or gender. He likes sports, I could care less. He likes hip-hop, I like jazz. I wondered what could he possibly bring to my life?

I later found out—everything.

Jefferson always saw me the way I wanted to be seen. He set the bar high and expected me to achieve it. I wanted to live up to his expectations so I rose to the occasion, even if I was scared in the process. I respected him, admired him, and never wanted to let him down. I've always done what he has asked of me, just to say—"Thank-you for believing in me."

I took action so often for him that I eventually wanted to do great things for myself too. Sometimes you see your value through your own eyes. Other times people see it for you, before you see it for yourself. This is the gift Jefferson gave me—the ability to look at myself and see wondrous things. His belief in me soon became my belief.

It first became real to me about a year after we really started working together. An important training event was coming up that I desperately wanted to attend. It cost several hundred dollars. Because I had just spent every dollar I had to cover my regular household bills, there was no money left.

Two days before the event, Jefferson called me and asked I was going. I said that I hadn't yet made arrangements. I wasn't sure if I could go, but I told him "anything was possible."

Then he said something that changed my life. He asked me, "Do you need any help?" (Do you need any money?)

There was no way he could have known. In that moment, I felt as if all eternity stood still. I saw myself as an eight-year-old again, asking for that lick of ice cream. I said to myself:

How can you say yes when you must never ask for help?

How can you say yes when it will show weakness?

How can you say yes when it reveal your neediness?

But I stood there and said, "Yes."

Because sometimes the strongest thing you can do is show that you are weak. Because sometimes the only way to move up, is to acknowledge that you are down. Because sometimes the only way God can put something in your hand, is to first make you acknowledge that it's empty.

When I said "Yes," I was so scared. I had never accepted help from anyone before. I had never opened up that part of me. But in that moment I told the eight-year-old little girl that is was okay to ask for some ice cream. I told her she didn't do anything wrong, and that her mom was just hurt. I told her that help is a gift from God.

I let myself trust my mentor who was also my friend. I let myself trust he would not hurt me with my own truth, my own vulnerability. I decided to let him inside my hard, tough shell.

His incredible act of kindness communicated I was worth the effort and the investment. Without a doubt, it was the beginning of my new life.

I discovered who I was at that training. I went from a timid woman afraid to get in the game, to a woman who now knows how to call the shots. I became the CEO of my own life. I became who I was called to be. And it all started because of that one simple question—"Do you need any help?"

With that question, we connect, we share, we grow, we love, we inspire. And when we have the courage to say "Yes," we let God do a work in us, because He made us to need each other. Give, and it shall be given unto you.

Thank you Jefferson for teaching me how to trust and how to receive.

About the Author

Jefferson Santos grew up in Richardson, Texas, with his mom and siblings. He attended and played football at the U.S. Naval Academy and Texas Christian University. Despite possessing great entrepreneurial ambition for a new start-up business, by the age of 20 life had him in a choke hold. His bank account was in the red at -$1,100 and his debt load of $70,000 told a similar tale.

Jefferson decided he needed a change.

With a newfound commitment, he turned that decision into a reality by discovering the Higher Life Design. Over time, this process helped him earn several million dollars and build a team of more than 100,000 leaders in over 30 countries.

He's since travelled the world and taken 107 vacations in 84 months. He's trained teams from New York to Singapore, Amsterdam to Zimbabwe, and everywhere else in between. An energetic and inspirational speaker, he's been blessed to share the stage with some of the biggest names in his industry—Dani Johnson, Brendon Burchard, Marcia Wieder, Cynthia Kersey, Loral Langemeier, Les Brown and Peter Diamandis.

Most importantly, Jefferson has been able to build schools in Guatemala and other regions in desperate need of resources. Through "VolunTourism" he's invested his time, talent, and treasures to those who need a hand up, not a hand out.

Jefferson shares the Higher Life Design with people who want to arrive at their intended destination healthy, wealthy, and happy. He and his wife, Megan, live in Texas with their two sons, Harrison and Livingston.

Arrive at your intended destination
healthy, wealthy, and happy.
Take your free Higher Life Design assessment.

HigherLifeDesign.com

Bring Jefferson to your next event.
Check his availability.

JeffersonSantos.com

ACKNOWLEDGMENTS

My Wife, Megan—

The respect and love you give me fuels me everyday. Your unwavering support and belief in me makes me aim to be even a better husband, father, and leader. You are my ultimate travel buddy and my Higher Life Design soul mate.

Wayne Nugent—

Thank you for taking me under your wing and being my mentor, my brother, and my friend. You have shown me how life is really meant to be lived. Your vision and passion for life inspires me daily. You truly are "A Master in the Art of Living."

Mike Azcue—

Your impact on me in the start of my career was bigger than you know. I have huge admiration for your strong character, excellence in execution, and unwavering integrity. You showed me the importance of personal development from the beginning.

Dani and Hans Johnson—

I owe a lot of my success to you. You influenced my teaching and showed me the power of consistent training. You are the epitome of the Higher Life Design. I respect and admire your impact on the world by educating people on faith, family, finances, and business.

Marc and Kelly Accetta—

Marc, you are one of the most gifted, talented, passionate, hard working, and humble people I know. I can't thank you enough for the energy you constantly pour into everyone. I have learned so much from you and I respect who you are and what you stand for.

Kelly, without your support Marc would not be able to do the things he does with such excellence. Thank you both!

Donovan Arterburn, Jr.—

Your teaching on excellence and follow-through was a pillar from the very start of my career. You've taught me the value of my own authenticity.

Robb and Kim Campbell—

I'm so impressed by your humility and teachability. It's fueled your massive success. You both have shown me unconditional friendship and have guided me through personal struggle.

Matt and Rhonda Morris, Johnny and Crystal Wimbrey—

I admire you for your example of how to lead a family. Your friendship for over a decade means the world to me. I am inspired by your confidence, expertise, and leadership.

Brad Cook—

In the beginning of my career, you helped me think outside of the box and expand my vision.

Mrs. Dooley (my seventh grade math teacher)—

Thank you for believing in me, pushing me to greatness at a young age. Because of you, I set a higher expectation of myself.

Mom—

You are my biggest cheerleader! I have always known you are proud of me and that my best is good enough for you. That is a gift to any son.

Dad and Ana—

Your standard of excellence challenged me to be better. Thank you for supporting me during the best time of my life.

Thank you, Ana, for your unconditional love and for keeping Dad in line all these years!

Jennifer, Kris, and Andrew—

Your love and support as siblings means so much to me.

Jared and Shannon Galligan, Kristina and David Waller, Scott and Sheila Ross, Thaddeus and Janice Whyte—

Your faith and foundation in Christ is evident. You've inspired me by your friendship and love for each other and the world.

Brendon Burchard—

Thank you for giving me so much clarity and defining what I'm capable of doing. You've paved the way with your expertise. I'm grateful for your mentorship and friendship.

Dan Stammen and Scotty Kufus—

You've raised the bar for entrepreneurs in our industry. I remember watching and admiring you from the crowd in 1998 when I was just getting my feet wet. I've learned so much from your strategies and tactics for success in life and in business. I'm so honored to call you friends.

Jon McKillip, Eddie Head, Kyle Lowe—

You are three amazing friends.

Jon, thank you for being a shining example on how to honor people by truly listening.

Eddie, your modeling behavior taught me that providing more value and direction consistently gives people the certainty and confidence they need to succeed.

Kyle, you've made it possible for me and my family to truly have friends abroad. You've taught me how to bring cultures from all over the world together.

Bob Wood—

Thank you for your long-time friendship. I've appreciated how you've taken my ideas and made them real.

My Football Coaches—

Tommy Robinson, Charlie Weatherbee, Gary Patterson, John Stoskoph, Ken Niumatalolo, Coach Boyd, Coach Dubey, and Coach Cox:

Thank you for pushing me to be better on and off of the field.

My Peers—

I wouldn't be where I am today if it wasn't for the support, camaraderie, and friendship of this group:

Byron Schrag, Jeff Bolf, Troy Brown, Dave Watson, David Pietsch, Martin Rouf, Dave and Yvette Ulloa, Dwight and Fadia Hanson, Kari and Lisha Schneider, Wes Melcher, Jeff Johnston, Maria DiPoce, Brian Dunivant, Carlos Rogers, Rob Flick, Dave Baird, Don Morton, Bethany Webster, Jeremy Larsen, Eric Gryzbowski, Gail Spears, Gaby Delgadillo, Mitch Blackford, and Chris and Rita Mayberry, Raymond and Janie Braun, Lorenzo Roybal, David Townsend, and Brian and Sarah Brown.

My Leaders—

A HUGE shout out and thank you to the leaders in my organization. Your hard work and dedication make it possible for me to serve and do what I do. Your impact will reach way beyond our lifetime.

Matt Morris, Johnny Wimbrey, Erlend Vatne, Eric "Happy" Gusevik, Peter Powderham, Shush Arya, Xristos Xristofi, Saavas Xristofi, Andreas Andreou, Katerina Konstantinou, Stavros Zenonos, James Lee, Dennis Bay, Sir Erwin, Amilee Kang, Soojay and Cassandra Devraj, Stavros Constantinides, Ed Blunt, Michael Jex, Julio Acosta, Jay Payso, Wendy Castillo, Sean Sturrock, Eric Allen, John Heerhold, Shelley Blanzy Colette Bowers, Ronnie Hodges, Deena Powers, Zach Edwards, Joe Thackery, Lisa Head, Daniel and Vanessa Rotoni, Toby Lemley, Srinivas Bhat, Stephen Lee, June Lee, April Consulo, Jay and Ashley Nelson, George Adamides, Efrosyni Adamides, Oz Koren, Michael Gurvich, Andreas Mamas, Rainer Zimmerman, Alexis-Astero Alexandrou, Reidar Furuholmen, Cynthia Koh, Craig Sweet, Carl and Sheryl Randolph, and Predrag Terzin.

My Internal Team—
Scarlett, Sarah, Jared, Clayton, Bob, and Kary—thank you for making me look good.

My Frequent International Travel Buddies—
Mike Putman, Monico Perez, and Courtney Tyler—thank you for always making my trips memorable.

My Naysayers—
You told me to get a real job. You told me I couldn't do it. Thank you for putting me up to the challenge. I used that as fuel to propel me to higher levels of thinking and being.

Notes

1 This quote has been widely attributed to many sources. However, based on our best research, we found it attributed to L. P. Jacks from his book written in 1932.

L. P. Jacks, *Education through recreation,* (New York: Harper & Brothers, 1932).

PART I: TAKEOFF—*Expectation*
Step One: Hungry for More

2 Brett McKay and Kate McKay, "How to Use Valet Parking (Without Looking Like an Idiot)", *The Art of Manliness* (blog), March 19, 2013, http://www.artofmanliness.com/2013/03/19/how-to-use-valet-parking-without-looking-like-an-idiot.

3 *Merriam-Webster OnLine,* s.v. "hunger", http://www.merriam-webster.com/dictionary/hunger.

4 Nature, "Cold Warriors: Wolves and Buffalo", *PBS* video, February 12, 2013, http://www.pbs.org/

wnet/nature/episodes/cold-warriors-wolves-and-buffalo/full-episode/8187.

5   Jeremiah 29:11

6   *The Free Dictionary by Farlex,* s.v. "decree", http://www.thefreedictionary.com/decree.

7   *Online Etymology Dictionary,* s.v. "decide", http://www.etymonline.com/index.php?term=decide.

8   Dan Ariely, *Predictably irrational,* (New York: Harper Collins, 2008).

9   Scott M. Fay, *Discover your sweet spot,* (New York: Morgan James, 2013).

Step Two: Pack Your Bags

10 *Merriam-Webster OnLine,* s.v. "baggage", http://www.merriam-webster.com/dictionary/baggage.

11 *The Free Dictionary by Farlex,* s.v. "baggage", http://www.thefreedictionary.com/baggage.

12 *Dictionary.com,* s.v. "luggage", http://dictionary.reference.com/browse/luggage.

13 Proverbs 16:18

14 Dr. Alan Goldberg, "The Athlete's Ego: Good or Bad?", *Competitive Advantage: Sports Psychology, Peak Performance, and Overcoming Fears & Blocks,* https://www.competitivedge.com/athlete's-ego-good-or-bad.

15 Associated Press, "Anderson Silva Knockout: Chris Weidman Wins Middleweight Title Fight at UFC 162", *The Huffington Post,* July 7, 2013, http://www.huffingtonpost.com/2013/07/07/

chris-wiedman-anderson-silva-ufc-162-
results_n_3556310.html.

16   Zig Ziglar, *Ziglar.com,* http://www.ziglar.com/
quotes/money-isnt-everything-it-ranks-right.

17   WorldVentures, "Giving Back", http://www.
worldventures.com/giving-back.

18   Experience Project, "I Need to Forgive Someone",
Experience Project (blog), May 29, 2008, http://
www.experienceproject.com/stories/Need-To-
Forgive-Someone/230846.

19   Betty W. Phillips, PhD., "The Secret Called
Forgiveness", http://www.bettyphillipspsychology.
com/id108.html.

20   Ibid.

21   Lewis B. Smedes, *Goodreads,* http://www.
goodreads.com/author/quotes/56576.Lewis_B_
Smedes.

22   Corrie ten Boom, "I'm Still Learning to Forgive",
Guideposts, 1972, quoted in Corrie ten Boom,
"Corrie ten Boom Story on Forgiving", *Family Life
Education,* http://www.familylifeeducation.org/
gilliland/procgroup/CorrieTenBoom.htm.

23   Ibid.

24   Roberto Assagioli, "Spiritual Practices:
Forgiveness", *Spirituality and Practice,* http://www.
spiritualityandpractice.com/practices/practices.
php?id=9&g=1.

25 *Wikipedia,* s.v. "millennials", last modified December 31, 2013, http://en.wikipedia.org/wiki/Millennials.

26 *Thesaurus.com,* s.v. "grumble", http://thesaurus.com/browse/grumble.

27 Elizabeth Scott, M.S., "Cortisol and Stress: How to Stay Healthy", *About.com,* updated October 18, 2013, http://stress.about.com/od/stresshealth/a/cortisol.htm.

28 For additional thoughts, see: Michael Hyatt, "#064: Two Kinds of Thinkers: Which One Are You?", *This is Your Life* (podcast), August 28, 2013, http://michaelhyatt.com/064-two-kinds-of-thinkers-podcast.html.

29 *The Free Dictionary by Farlex,* s.v. "envy", http://www.thefreedictionary.com/envy.

30 "Inspirational Quotations", *Appreciative Inquiry Commons,* http://appreciativeinquiry.case.edu/practice/quotes.cfm.

31 Kathy Caprino, "Millionaire Brendon Burchard Shares the One Most Important Trait 'Experts' Need to Succeed", *Forbes,* June 27, 2012, http://www.forbes.com/sites/kathycaprino/2012/06/27/millionaire-brendon-burchard-shares-the-one-most-important-trait-experts-need-to-succeed/.

32 Sheryl Paul, "Love is a Verb", *The Huffington Post,* October 15, 2012, http://www.huffingtonpost.com/sheryl-paul/love-is-a-verb_1_b_1940731.html.

33 Dr. Valerie Young, "What Every Woman (and Man) Needs to Know about Competence, the Imposter Syndrome, and the Art of Winging It." PAESMEM Stanford School of Engineering Workshop, May 9, 2005, http://paesmem.stanford.edu/html/proceedings_8.html.

34 David Graham, "The Imposter Syndrome: Behind the Mask", *Toronto Star,* (website), July 14, 2007, http://www.thestar.com/article/234422.

35 Dr. Valerie Young, "What Every Woman (and Man) Needs to Know about Competence, the Imposter Syndrome, and the Art of Winging It." PAESMEM Stanford School of Engineering Workshop, May 9, 2005, http://paesmem.stanford.edu/html/proceedings_8.html.

36 "Be Kind; Everyone You Meet is Fighting a Hard Battle," *Quote Investigator,* June 29, 2010, http://quoteinvestigator.com/2010/06/29/be-kind.

37 Andy Wachowski and Lana Wachowski, *The Matrix,* motion picture, directed by Andy Wachowski and Lana Wachowski (The Wachowski Brothers), (1999, USA: Warner Bros.).

and

J. R. R. Tolkien, Fran Walsh, Philippa Boyens, Peter Jackson, *The Lord of the Rings: The Fellowship of the Ring,* motion picture, directed by Peter Jackson, (2001, USA: New Line Cinema)

38 *The Free Dictionary by Farlex,* s.v. "gutsy", http://www.thefreedictionary.com/gutsy.

39   *Wikipedia,* s.v. "William Wallace", last modified
      December 24, 2013, http://en.wikipedia.org/wiki/
      William_Wallace.

40   Richard LaGravenese, Freedom Writers, and Erin
      Gruwell, *Freedom Writers,* motion picture, directed
      by Richard LaGravenese, (2007, USA: Paramount
      Pictures).

41   "Leading Thoughts: Quotes on Self-Discipline",
      Leadership Now, http://www.leadershipnow.com/
      disciplinequotes.html.

42   Darren Hardy, "Do You Have a Fat Head?", *Darren
      Hardy,* August 6, 2013, http://darrenhardy.success.
      com/2013/08/do-you-have-a-fat-head.

43   OptimaHealth, "Optima EAP Thought of the
      Week", July 28, 2008, https://www.jlab.org/div_
      dept/admin/HR/EAP/07-28-08.pdf.

44   Elle, "The Biggest Losers: Battle of the Fad Diets",
      Elle, (website), May 24, 2013, http://www.elle.
      com/beauty/health-fitness/most-popular-fad-
      diets#slide-2.

45   Mark Sisson, "Primal Blueprint 101", *Mark's Daily
      Apple* (blog), http://www.marksdailyapple.com/
      primal-blueprint-101.
      and Loren Cordain, PhD, *The Paleo Diet*, http://
      thepaleodiet.com.

46   Stanley Bronstein, "Change Your Life – Law #24 –
      Position Yourself to be Disciplined", *SuperChange
      Your Life* (blog), April 29, 2013, http://
      superchangeyourlife.com/change-your-life-law24.

47   Anne Marie Helmenstine, PhD, "How Much of Your Body is Water?", *About.com,* http://chemistry. about.com/od/waterchemistry/f/How-Much-Of-Your-Body-Is-Water.htm.

48   Liza Barnes and Nicole Nichols, "Eat More Often, Lose More Weight: The Benefits of Eating Several Small Meals Each Day", SparkPeople, http:// www.sparkpeople.com/resource/nutrition_articles. asp?id=1144.

49   Dr James B. Maas, Megan L. Wherry, David J. Axelrod, Barbara R. Hogan, and Jennifer A. Blumen, "Learning About the Power of Sleep", *Power sleep: the revolutionary program that prepares your mind for peak performance,* (New York: The New York Times on the Web, 1998) http://www. nytimes.com/books/first/m/maas-sleep.html.

50   Ibid.

51   Ibid.

52   Eric Hoffer, *The Ordeal of Change,* (1963).

53   *Wikiquote,* s.v. "Anatole France", last modified September 20, 2013, http://en.wikiquote.org/wiki/ Anatole_France.

54   John C. Maxwell, *The 21 irrefutable laws of leadership: follow them and people will follow you,* (Nashville: Thomas Nelson, 1997).

55   *searchQuotes,* s.v. "Charles DuBois", http://www. searchquotes.com/quotation/The_important_ thing_is_this%3A_To_be_able_at_any_moment_

to_sacrifice_what_we_are_for_what_we_could_
bec/301242.

56   *Thinkexist.com,* http://thinkexist.com/quotation/
tell_me_and_i-ll_forget-show_me_and_i_
may/10546.html.

PART II: FLIGHT—*Preparation*
Step Three: The Attitude Equation

57   D. L. Stewart., *Dayton Daily News,* quoted by
Nyad Xtreme Dream, http://www.diananyad.com/
diana.

58   *Wikipedia,* s.v. "Diana Nyad", last modified
December 30, 2013, http://en.wikipedia.org/wiki/
Diana_Nyad.

59   Michael Walsh, "Diana Nyad reveals what was
going through her head during 53-hour 'Xtreme
dream' swim", *NYDailyNews,* (website), September
4, 2013, http://www.nydailynews.com/news/
national/diana-nyad-opens-xtreme-dream-swim-
cuba-florida-article-1.1445880#ixzz2e2lfi2zW.

60   Cory Edwards, "Lessons in Manliness: Viktor
Frankl", *The Art of Manliness* (blog), August 8,
2008, http://www.artofmanliness.com/2008/08/08/
profiles-in-manliness-viktor-frankl.

61   Viktor E. Frankl, *Man's search for meaning,* (Vienna,
Austria: 1946; USA: 1959).

62   John C. Maxwell, "Fight for Your Dreams in
2011", *John Maxwell on Leadership* (blog), Januarry
3, 2011, adapted from John C. Maxwell, *Put your*

dream to the test: 10 questions that will help you see it and seize it, (Nashville: Thomas Nelson, 2009), http://johnmaxwellonleadership.com/2011/01/03/fight-for-your-dreams-in-2011.

63   Katherine Jacobsen, "Why Diana Nyad refused to let her 'Xtreme Dream' die", *The Christian Science Monitor* (website), September 3, 2013, http://www.csmonitor.com/USA/USA-Update/2013/0903/Why-Diana-Nyad-refused-to-let-her-Xtreme-Dream-die-video.

64   Matt Sloane, Jason Hanna, and Dana Ford, "'Never give up:' Diana Nyad completes historic, Cuba-to-Florida swim", *CNN* (website), September 3, 2013, http://www.cnn.com/2013/09/02/world/americas/diana-nyad-cuba-florida-swim.

65   *Nyad Xtreme Dream,* http://www.diananyad.com.

66   Matt Pearce, "Diana Nyad, after swim: 'You're never too old to chase your dreams'", *Los Angeles Times* (website), September 3, 2013, http://www.latimes.com/nation/nationnow/la-na-nn-diana-nyad-cuba-florida-remarks-20130902,0,1729111.story.

67   CBS News, "Diana Nyad on epic swim: My mantra was 'find a way'", *CBS News* (website), September 3, 2013, http://www.cbsnews.com/news/diana-nyad-on-epic-swim-my-mantra-was-find-a-way.

68   "Ernistine Shepard the 75 Year Old Bodybuilding Grandma", YouTube video, 2:54, posted by

"Beanyman62News", July 11, 2012, http://www. youtube.com/watch?v=aUS0mrnMG0k.

69   Nick Vujicic, *Life Without Limbs,* http://www. lifewithoutlimbs.org.

Step Four: Change Your Story

70   *Wikipedia,* s.v. "hakuna matata", last modified December 31, 2013, http://en.wikipedia.org/wiki/ Hakuna_matata.

71   Irene Mecchi and Jonathan Roberts, *The Lion King,* motion picture, directed by Roger Allers and Rob Minkoff (Buena Vista Pictures,1994; Walt Disney Home Video, 2011), DVD.

72   John 8:32

73   Irene Mecchi and Jonathan Roberts, *The Lion King,* motion picture, directed by Roger Allers and Rob Minkoff (Buena Vista Pictures,1994; Walt Disney Home Video, 2011), DVD.

74   Ibid.

75   Ibid.

Step Five: The First Class Formula

76   State Farm Mutual Automobile Insurance Company, "Steering Wheel Hand Position", *Teen Driver Safety,* last modified April 8, 2013, http:// teendriving.statefarm.com/teaching-a-teen-to-drive/ being-a-role-model/steering-wheel-hand-position.

77   K. A. Ericsson, R. Th. Krampe, and C. Tesch-Romer, "The role of deliberate practice in the acquisition of expert performance", *Psychological Review,* 100 (1993), 393–4.

78   Deirdre Donahue, "Malcolm Gladwell's 'Success' defines 'outlier' achievement", *USA Today* (website), last modified November 18, 2008, http://usatoday30.usatoday.com/life/books/news/2008-11-17-gladwell-success_N.htm.

79   This quote has been widely attributed to many sources. However, based on our best research, we found it attributed to L. P. Jacks from his book written in 1932.
      L. P. Jacks, *Education through recreation,* (New York: Harper & Brothers, 1932).

80   Darren Hardy, "Why the Rich Get Richer", *Darren Hardy* (blog), November 8, 2011, http://darrenhardy.success.com/2011/11/why-the-rich-get-richer.

81   Proverbs 11:14

82   *WikiHow,* "How to Get an Upgrade to First Class", http://www.wikihow.com/Get-an-Upgrade-to-First-Class.

83   Ibid.

84   Proverbs 23:7

PART III: LANDING—*Integration*
Step Six: Celebrate the Moment

85   *The Free Dictionary by Farlex,* s.v. "dissociation", http://www.thefreedictionary.com/dissociation.

86   *Wikipeida,* s.v. "dissociation", http://en.wikipedia.org/wiki/Dissociation_(psychology).

87   Gallup, Inc., http://www.gallup.com, accessed June
     30, 2013.

88   Kelli Grant, "Americans hate their jobs and even
     perks don't help," *Today/NBC News,* June 24, 2013,
     http://www.today.com/money/americans-hate-
     their-jobs-even-perks-dont-help-6C10423977.

89   The engagement levels in China, Singapore, and
     Germany are much worse than the United States.
     See: Marco Nink, "Employee Disengagement
     Plagues Germany", *Gallup Business Journal*
     (website), April 9, 2009, http://businessjournal.
     gallup.com/content/117376/employee-
     disengagement-plagues-germany.aspx.
     Ashok Gopal, "Worker Disengagement Continues
     to Cost Singapore", *Gallup Business Journal*
     (website), May 11, 2006, http://businessjournal.
     gallup.com/content/22720/worker-disengagement-
     continues-cost-singapore.aspx.
     Jim Clifton, "China, We Have a Workforce
     Problem", *Gallup Business Journal* (website),
     February 21, 2013, http://businessjournal.gallup.
     com/content/160406/china-workplace-problem.
     aspx.

90   Kelli Grant, "Americans hate their jobs and even
     perks don't help," *Today/NBC News,* June 24, 2013,
     http://www.today.com/money/americans-hate-
     their-jobs-even-perks-dont-help-6C10423977.

91   "Billionaires' Advice for New College Grads,"
     Forbes (website), http://www.forbes.com/pictures/

edek45fghe/steve-jobs-live-each-day-as-if-it-was-your-last.

92 Darren Hardy, "The Vault Door is Open!", *Darren Hardy* (blog), June 4, 2013, http://darrenhardy. success.com/2013/06/the-vault-door-is-open.

93 Martin Hilbert and Priscila Lopez, "The world's technological capacity to process information", *MartinHilbert.net* (blog), http://www.martinhilbert. net/WorldInfoCapacity.html.

94 Marcia Conner, "Data on Big Data", *MarciaConner. com* (blog), July 18, 2012, http://marciaconner. com/blog/data-on-big-data.

95 Blaise Pascal, *Pensées and other writings,* (Oxford: Oxford University Press, 1995).

96 *Wikiquote,* s.v. "Talk: Thomas Edison", last modified June 13, 2013, http://en.wikiquote.org/ wiki/Talk:Thomas_Edison.

97 Mark Sisson, "The Physiological Consequences of Being Hyperconnected", *Mark's Daily Apple* (blog), October 10, 2013, http://www.marksdailyapple. com/the-physiological-consequences-of-being-hyperconnected.

98 Alice G. Walton, "Internet Addiction: The New Mental Health Disorder?", *Forbes* (website), October 2, 2012, http://www.forbes.com/sites/ alicegwalton/2012/10/02/the-new-mental-health-disorder-internet-addiction.

99 David Rock, "Your Brain on Facebook", *Harvard Business Review HBR Blog Network* (blog), May 18,

2012, http://blogs.hbr.org/2012/05/your-brain-on-facebook.

100 Mark Sisson, "The Physiological Consequences of Being Hyperconnected", *Mark's Daily Apple* (blog), October 10, 2013, http://www.marksdailyapple.com/the-physiological-consequences-of-being-hyperconnected.

101 Blaise Pascal, *Pensées and other writings,* (Oxford: Oxford University Press, 1995).

102 James Fieser (editor), "The Matrix (1999)," *Philosophical Films,* http://www.philfilms.utm.edu/1/matrix.htm.

103 "Apple Steve Jobs The Crazy Ones – NEVER BEFORE AIRED 1997", YouTube video, 1:01, posted by "S Jackson", February 1, 2009, http://www.youtube.com/watch?v=8rwsuXHA7RA.

104 Ibid.

105 *Wikipedia,* s.v. "Think Different, last modified December 30, 2013, http://en.wikipedia.org/wiki/Think_Different.

Step Seven: The Integration Effect

106 *The Free Dictionary by Farlex,* s.v. "great oaks from little acorns grow", http://idioms.thefreedictionary.com/Great+oaks+from+little+acorns+grow.

107 Peter Gosling, "Fascinating Tree Seed Facts", *The Tree Seed Consultant*, http://www.treeseedconsultant.co.uk/average-seeds-per-tree.html.

108 Ibid.

109 "Attitudes of creative people: A descriptive sketch of the creative person", *Innovation Management,* http://www.innovationmanagement.se/imtool-articles/attitudes-of-creative-people-a-descriptive-sketch-of-the-creative-person.

110 MG Siegler, "Eric Schmidt: Every 2 Days We Create As Much Information As We Did Up To 2003", August 4, 2010, http://techcrunch.com/2010/08/04/schmidt-data.

111 Joe Kraus, "We're creating a culture of distraction", May 25, 2012, http://joekraus.com/were-creating-a-culture-of-distraction.

112 Denis Campbell, "Email stress – the new office workers' plague: A deluge of messages distracts people from work", August 11, 2007, *The Observer / The Guardian* (website), http://www.theguardian.com/technology/2007/aug/12/news.

113 MG Siegler, "Eric Schmidt: Every 2 Days We Create As Much Information As We Did Up To 2003", August 4, 2010, http://techcrunch.com/2010/08/04/schmidt-data.

114 "'Infomania' worse than marijuana", April 22, 2005, http://news.bbc.co.uk/2/hi/uk_news/4471607.stm

115 Peter Bregman, "How (and Why) to Stop Multitasking", *Harvard Business Review HBR Blog Network* (blog), May 20, 2010, http://blogs.hbr.org/2010/05/how-and-why-to-stop-multitaski.

116 "The law of gender guarantees our goals to become real", http://www.creative-wealthbuilding.com/law-of-gender.html.
and
Bob Proctor, "Universal Law of Gender", *Purpose Balance Life,* http://www.purposebalancelife.com/law-of-gender.html.

Arrive at your intended destination
healthy, wealthy, and happy.
Take your free Higher Life Design assessment.

HigherLifeDesign.com

Bring Jefferson to your next event.
Check his availability.

JeffersonSantos.com

CPSIA information can be obtained at www.ICGtesting.com
Printed in the USA
LVOW07s1827171014

409312LV00003B/101/P